ELDER TALES

Spirited women over sixty tell their stories

by

Ruth Garrison

and

Lorry Roberts

Compiled by

Soroptimist International of Boise

in honor of their 60th Anniversary

Historic Idaho, Inc. • Boise, Idaho

Library of Congress Control No. 00-134637
International Standard Book Number (ISBN): 0-9631258-5-0

First Edition

Original cover artwork and interior illustrations by Ruth Barnes Kunze

Edited by Jean M. Terra

Interviews and copyediting by Marilee Cross and Tyce Lind,
Boise State University Interns

Design & Layout by Richard Terra / Terra Nova

Published by:
Historic Idaho, Inc.
P.O. Box 4534
Boise, Idaho 83711

Printed in the United States of America
Writer's Press, Inc.
Boise, Idaho USA

Soroptimist International of Boise will be sixty years old on October 12, 2000. To celebrate our 60th Anniversary, we have written sixty stories about sixty women over the age of sixty. Our hope is that these stories will live on as a record of women's achievements and their important place in history. We are grateful to Historic Idaho, Inc. for their funding.

Soroptimist International is a worldwide organization for women in management and professions working through service projects to advance human rights and the status of women. It all began in Oakland, California, on October 3, 1921, when the first Soroptimist Club was formed. Violet Richardson-Ward was installed as the Club's first President with eighty members present. By 1926, Soroptimist clubs had been formed in San Francisco, Los Angeles, Sacramento, Long Beach, San Jose, New York, Washington DC, Vancouver BC, London and France. By 1939, there were ninety-one clubs with 4,500 members in America. Soroptimist clubs in Europe struggled to form as World War II raged on. Today, Soroptimist International is the world's largest classified service organization for women with over 95,000 members in over 3,000 clubs in 120 countries.

Soroptimist International of Boise was chartered on October 12, 1940, with twenty charter members. Dues during that first year were two dollars a month, which included the cost of one luncheon and one dinner. Leah B. Flack was our first President. During that first year, members voted to sponsor a tea service for the light cruiser USS Boise, which saw heavy action in the Pacific during World War II. This silver tea service is still on display in the city of Boise mayor's office. We are proud to have one of our charter members and fourth club president, Fern-Lucille Sawyer, still attending club functions. In the past sixty years, members have participated in countless service projects locally, nationally and internationally. However, those first members initiated service projects that still continue today. One project began by giving gifts to patients in the County Hospital. When the hospital was torn down in 1957, the Christmas gifts were given to nursing home patients. Last year, over 875 nursing home residents and 348 foster children received Christmas gifts through this program.

There have been many changes since those early years, but one thing remains the same: the spirit of those first women who dared to make a difference. I hope that you will find the same spirit in these stories.

Jan Hall
Soroptimist International of Boise
2000-2001 President

Preface

There are so many other Idaho women who could have been in this book, who embodied the standards of greatness in the everyday that the women in this book represent, and that gives this generation its special quality and distinction. Those over sixty years of age have known many challenges and many joys. They have learned coping skills that have carried them through life. It is our hope that this book will validate those women, as well as be an inspiration to younger people to learn from them, to set goals, dream big and follow those dreams.

Ruth Garrison & Lorry Roberts

Foreword

Ask a successful woman how she has made her way and she will likely advocate good cheer and perseverance, as you might expect. Ask where that started in her life and she may speak of an aunt, a teacher, her mother, grandmother. In each culture and every age, women have given each other skills, encouragement, a song, guiding words of advice. In our country of immigrants, with so much that was strange and new, these legacies were enormously important.

Today, as young women look for their place in a world that is stranger and newer every day, the wise words of elders seem farther away than ever. Lorry Roberts, Ruth Garrison and Soroptimist International of Boise have responded by collecting the stories of many women who have found a way to live with dignity and generosity among us.

There are two gifts here. Each story, all by itself, is enchanting, like an afternoon with a modest and remarkable woman. One shares stories of her mother, her grandmother, and her great-grandmother. One teaches cooking and the songs of a country and language she once left far behind. Another, rather casually, speaks of earning her pilot's license after a long, productive and very different professional career. With a little early support to light their way, these women kept their feet under them, even when life sent them on unexpected paths.

Here, in other words, are many lights. This collection is an opportunity to have many aunts, many encouraging mothers and friends. This book is a virtual loving community.

And that's the second gift. After reading this book, who will see the white-haired woman in the checkout line the same way? How many will be inspired to volunteer some time, speak up, help out, give back to the strong and generous women all around us?

Jeanette Ross, Ed.D
Project Director
Boise 2000 Lasting Legacy Project
"Boise By Heart"
Memories of the 1950s

Acknowledgments

Sincere thanks to Ruth Barnes Kunze for her creative cover artwork and interior illustrations.

We appreciate the efforts of GaNeille Posey, Shirley Hill, Kitty Dooley, Bev Ross and Lorie Icenhower for their one-on-one interviewing.

*An alphabetical listing of the stories
appears in the index beginning on page 267.*

Elder Tales

Many people will walk in and out of your life, but only true friends will leave footprints on your heart.

— Eleanor Roosevelt

Fern Lucille Sawyer

"Take time to be yourself
and to know your family and friends."

When Fern Lucille's children asked her to write down the story of her life, she didn't think it would be possible. Her life has been so full that she couldn't even think how to start. "So many things have happened in my life." Then she had a dream in which her late husband Don told her that her life story would be easy if she just divided it into each decade:

1912-1921: a little girl growing up in Caldwell and Boise
1922-1931: a high school girl who then takes over a studio
1932-1941: a businesswoman and artist
1942-1951: marriage and children
1952-1961: children complete school, mother dies
1962-1971: husband is sick, nurses him for eleven years

Don died in 1974. This was the hardest event in her life. Since then she has been alone but not lonely.

Her earliest memory of her father's portrait business: at age four or five, she would sit with the family whose portrait was to be taken, helping to put them at ease with this new experience, while her father prepared to take the photo. When he was ready, she would then move out of the way. Her father's business was very successful and she always watched him work. He used glass negatives and put silver on the plates. She says she always knew she wanted to be a photographer. When she was seven, in 1919, the house and studio were built at 13th and State in Boise, where it still is located today. Her father's motto was displayed in the new studio: "The difference between a stepping stone and a stumbling block is the way you use it."

Fern Lucille's father wanted her to have an art education, as he felt this was important for a photographer. She was ready to attend a photography school in France when she finished high school in 1930. Instead, at the age of seventeen, she took over the family photography business due to her father's illness. During the 1930s, it was called the "Fern Lucille Burns Studio." She had a couple of the employees, and her mother and father helped when they could. She enjoyed working with people, especially the children. She got to know whole families as she recorded the events in their lives: graduations, weddings, and births. During the Depression there was little money for photographs and Fern Lucille was paid with chickens, eggs, milk, vegetables and housecleans.

After submitting a portfolio of her portraits, Fern Lucille was chosen to attend the Ansel Adams Master Class in Los Angeles in the summer of 1939. Of the 100 photographers who attended, only six were women. "I was one of the original libbers," Fern Lucille said.

In 1940, Fern Lucille was taking photographs for *The Idaho Statesman* Society page. She was asked to join Soroptimist International of Boise, a newly formed service organization for professional women. When she was serving as president, she announced that she would have to resign due to pregnancy. The board would not allow her to resign. Not only did they find nothing in the by-laws forbidding a pregnant president, the whole club acted as "aunties" to the baby and insisted that Fern Lucille bring the baby to the club meetings.

In 1942, she married Donald Sawyer after several years of dating, during which they attended dressy dances and charity balls, the picture shows and dined at the Owyhee Plaza and Idanha Hotels. She says the secret to their good marriage was being good friends before they were married. They had two children, Sharon in 1945, and John in 1951.

She continued working until 1943 when photographic supplies became hard to get during the war. She gave her share of the available supplies to the two other photographers in Boise and closed the business for the remainder of the war years. The lenses were kept safe at the bank. By the end of the war, Fern Lucille had started a family and her younger brother, Stanley Martin Burns, had returned from the Navy. He reopened the business, which still today is called Burns Studio.

Fern Lucille Sawyer was a Charter Member of Soroptimist International of Boise. She still attends all the group's meetings, and is the 'light' of our lives.

You may encounter many defeats
but you must not be defeated.

— Maya Angelou

Marilyn Watts

"Life will go on regardless of how difficult it may seem at the moment."

I was a young child during the Depression. My memories are of being poor, but I didn't know it because everyone else also was poor. Looking back, I know I was poor but never hungry. I lived on a farm in Minnesota and there was always food, maybe only bread and potatoes, but there was food.

I was eight years old and had braids secured with rubber bands. I broke a rubber band and went to the place where we kept them, which was the mouthpiece of the wall telephone. There were none. My mother asked if I had broken my rubber band and when I told her I had, she said there were no more. We had no money buy them and had them only if some produce happened to have a rubber band on it. So I had to find some string to tie the end of my braids.

I attended a one-room school and had the same teacher for my fourth through eighth grades. I can credit her for my good grammar and reading skills and my love of reading. My high school band teacher taught me to appreciate classical music and my high school English teacher brought Shakespeare and other great authors to life.

My career has been nursing and hospice, starting when I graduated in 1954. I applied for my first job with the U.S. Public Health Service as a nurse in Mt. Edgecombe, a part of the Alaskan Territory. I worked in the children's orthopedic wing of the tuberculosis hospital. Most of the children couldn't speak English when they came but quickly learned as they adapted to life and school in that hospital. I met a nurse there from North Dakota. We became good friends and decided our next move would be to apply to Standard Oil for a job in Arabia as the oil companies were hiring nurses for overseas jobs at the time.

On the third day I was in Alaska, I met Steve Watts, who was a commercial fisherman. Our marriage took place in Minnesota in 1956 and then we went to California where I worked in a physician's office for a year. It was then on to Idaho, where we still live. I applied for a job at Sacred Heart Hospital and worked as a staff nurse and house supervisor for about sixteen years.

My career became part-time while having and raising our three children, two boys and a girl. Because of hospital politics, I became the leader in an employee battle to fight for nursing care for the patients. The hospital was no longer a caring, friendly Catholic Hospital; the financial bottom line ruled and nursing positions were cut. We lost the fight. I became disenfranchised and left the hospital to work in a nursing home. While there, the administrator approached me about starting a hospice, a concept I was interested in. I started the hospice and watched it grow into a successful program that I ran until my retirement in 1995.

I went back to school when my youngest child left for college and got my degree in health care administration. It was probably a more interesting experience than it would have been if I had done it when I was young, and had very few life experiences.

My biggest challenge was running the hospice program. In the early days, there were no how-to books. As the first one in the community, I was always charting new courses. The hospice had a membership in the National Hospice Organization and I learned much from talking with other people; it was hospices helping hospices. The work is very intense and taking care of the staff to avoid burnout was a big challenge.

The hardest thing I faced in my life was being told I had cancer. Life can never be the same after hearing the words, "You have a malignancy." I learned to not sweat the small stuff. I had surgery over twenty-five years ago and I feel very fortunate. I was really reminded of my good fortune when I cared for my first hospice patient, a woman who was born in the same town and in the same year I was born, and who had the same kind of cancer I had had. When she died, I had to ask, "Why her and not me?"

The biggest turning points in my life have been having children, changing churches and retirement. I was a career person until my first child was born. When he was a few weeks old and I was feeling normal again, I arranged to go back to work at the hospital on the night shift. I took the baby with me in a car bed; he slept in the linen closet, woke up early in the morning to be fed, then went back to sleep while I finished my shift.

During my hospice years, I watched many people die with varying degrees of faith from no faith in a supreme being to devout believers in Christianity, Judaism and Buddhism. I decided there was no right religion and there was no wrong one unless it taught intolerance to other belief systems or lifestyles. So I found the Unitarian Church which has no "belief system" but has principles which include respect for the worth and dignity of every human being. I am very comfortable with that philosophy.

For years, I couldn't imagine living without hospice; it was my baby of sorts. But the day came when I could not do what I wanted to do because of working under a parent company. So I made the decision to leave and when I walked out of my office doors for the last time, I never had any regrets.

Since then, I have been actively involved in organizing a new hospice, in keeping with the national guidelines. I am President of the Board of Directors and we expect to be up and running by the fall of 2000.

One very important thing I have learned in my lifetime is Maslov's hierarchy of needs, with food and shelter being at the core of life's necessities. If those two are present, anyone can survive quite well without the myriad of inventions that have made our lives more comfortable. I think power outages are good for society; they force people to realize that life can go on without electricity.

What I would like people to know about me is that I am a very caring person. I can have empathy for most situations and have the ability to say the right thing in difficult situations. I do not avoid unpleasant circumstances involving people and know that life will go on regardless of how difficult it may seem at the moment.

Miriam Barr

"I am concerned about whether I turned the wrong corner at some point."

When I was a junior at Meridian High School, I decided that I wanted to be a newspaper reporter. Why that occupation came to me, I do not know. Inez Calloway Robb, who was reared in Caldwell, was my idol. At that time, she was a foreign correspondent for an international news service, covering the politics and rumblings of war in Europe.

I asked John Baird, then owner, publisher and (other than his wife) sole reporter of the weekly *Meridian Times,* if I could write about high school news for the paper. He agreed and I was paid a dollar a week for my work, which included other chores around the shop.

Then I attended Boise Junior College for two years, the first two years at BJC's new campus, from 1940 to 1942. I edited the school's paper, *The Round-Up,* in the winter and spring terms of my freshman year, and I edited *Les Bois,* the yearbook, in my sophomore year. Upon graduation from BJC, I was hired, July 2, 1942, as a proofreader for *The Idaho Statesman.* I later became a reporter, a job that subsequently lasted 45 years.

In April 1944, I began reporting in Nampa and was assigned back and forth between Boise and Canyon County, as well as Murphy, Marsing and Homedale in Owyhee County, and Payette, Washington, Gem and Malheur counties.

I was born July 21, 1922, in Boise, the first of three children of William and Lillie Curtis. My father was a veteran of World War I, and a member of the Idaho National Guard Cavalry where he worked as a horseshoer. My mother had worked as a clerk at the Golden Rule store for C.C. Anderson, but was a homemaker after her marriage.

My sister, Marguerite, was also born in Boise. When she was just past a year old, our family moved to a small farm near Meridian, where my brother Bill was born. A couple of years after the move to Meridian, the stables at the Federal Reserve barracks burned, along with more than 100 head of horses, including my father's saddle horse and a number of prized polo ponies. It was a great tragedy that took my father's income, right at the time of the Depression.

When I was a second grader, an apparent epidemic of smallpox swept this area. All of the students were notified to get vaccinated. The vaccine didn't take on me and several days later, I became lethargic, was bent over at the waist, and slept much of the day and night. Many years later, a physician told me that the symptoms I described were similar to what could be a mild case of a combination of spinal meningitis, poliomyelitis and encephalitis. It left me, after about seven weeks, with round shoulders, poor posture and possibly other results (dulled my brain — ha).

I was the only woman reporter in the news department for a number of years. The Society department employed all women but the straight news department did not. There was quite a bit of employee turnover, and some firing now and then. I used to wonder if I would be next. Then I thought that the reason I didn't get fired was because I didn't cost them much. The men were paid more for covering the same kinds of stories. At times, when I would think about the difference in money, I would be angry or jealous, but then I would forget about it until the next time. For most of the years, I worked a swing shift, which prevented me from socializing. I didn't marry until I was past thirty and the marriage did not last long. But life goes on!

Most of my reminiscing goes back to my 20s and 30s, which takes me to the war years. While I was proofreading, I read all about the war. I have memories of servicemen I met during World War II. I have also met the first three persons released from Hunt Relocation Center northeast of Twin Falls, which was one of several internment camps for persons of Japanese ancestry. The three young men obtained work as night bellhops at the former Hotel Boise, which was one block east of the Greyhound Bus Depot. The only restaurant open to the three men for their mid-shift meal (about 3 A.M.) was the bus depot cafe because the bus depot had to accept everyone, regardless of race. I saw the dirty looks the men were given by people as they got off the buses and this made me angry. So I smiled at them each night as I waited for a bus to take me home to Meridian and friendships grew.

Memories of the forties were rekindled in the sixties when I worked in Caldwell and the closest restaurant was a lunch counter in a billiard parlor operated by a Japanese-American family. I became a friend to that family and soon I was a member of the Japanese American Citizens League.

Looking back on what has become a long life — and I'm not through yet — events just melded until I have to be satisfied. If only I had someone along throughout the years to remind me to choose wisely. I have become more active in the United Methodist Church on the regional level; United Methodist Women; Order of the Eastern Star;

and Daughters of the Nile. I have concentrated on trying to raise flowers and grass without weeds. I have more time than ever to read for myself, and I want to continue as long as I have good health.

My sister has two daughters, and each of them has two daughters of her own. My brother has a daughter and a son and five grandchildren. So I have youth in life.

I have had a long life (and I'm not through yet). The events of my life have taken shape and I realize that I must be satisfied with the results. It is up to the choices we make in life whether we are satisfied. It is up to us.

Shizue Abo

"Wealth isn't measured in money but in service helping out the less fortunate."

My grandma Shiz was born on March 24, 1923, in Idaho Falls, Idaho, and is full Japanese. Her parents, Tsura and Yokichi Nishizaki, came over from Japan before she was born. She had six brothers and five sisters. One sister died in a fire at a very young age, one brother died of a sickness at the age of three, and another brother died of heart problems. She has three sisters and two brothers alive today.

My grandma wore one dress all week to school because she was poor, and that's all she had after the fire. It was also during the Great Depression. She was very sensitive about not having too much money and said that kids would make fun of her all the time. They couldn't afford Valentines for everyone so they would save the ones they got, erase them and use them over. She took a bath once a week in a wash-tub. She very seldom went to a movie, although it only cost five cents. On a good Christmas she would get an orange or some nuts. Her family would decorate the Christmas tree with popcorn. She played games with her brothers and sisters such as jacks, jump rope or digging a hole in the ground and trying to roll the ball into the hole. Every

Saturday night when they got the paper, my grandma would look forward to reading the funnies.

My grandma got a job working for her teacher washing clothes and doing other jobs for twenty-five cents an hour. At home she would weed and pick the garden and help her mom fix dinner. She attended high school in Glenns Ferry, playing basketball for the school; her team won a State Championship.

"Winter was hard," she said, "especially living in a two room house."

Her father died when she was seventeen. It had a big impact on her family, her mother took it very hard, and it put a tremendous responsibility on her oldest brother, Tom, to help raise the family and take care of the farm.

After that, she decided to do good in life. She went to college and later became a registered nurse. "One of my most memorable moments," she said, "was when I was accepted to Nursing School." She started work at Margaret Hague, the largest maternity hospital in the world at that time. She later met my grandpa George at a picnic; she saw him off and on after that and they were married in 1949.

My grandma's childhood was very hard but she made it through. Today her hobbies are sewing, cooking and fishing with my grandpa. My grandparents recently celebrated their 50th wedding anniversary. My grandma had five children (two boys and three girls) and now has nine grandchildren. Her advice is "Wealth isn't measured in money but

in service helping out the less fortunate." She's very, very giving and caring, always making things for others such as sleeping bags for the homeless and blankets for people in the Oklahoma City bombing. She is always at church on Sunday. She said that her mother always made her go to Sunday school and that church really helped her.

Shizue's granddaughter, Linsey Abo, wrote this story when she was twelve years old. She is now fourteen, and very proud to have a grandmother like Shiz.

Character—the willingness to accept responsibility for one's own life—is the source from which self-respect springs.

— Joan Didion

Shirley Randolph

"We earn the privilege of living each day and surrender it as one full lifetime."

I was born in 1931 to a farming family in the mountains of Colorado, the youngest of three girls. It was in the Depression, but we were never hungry because we had our own meat, eggs, chickens, milk and vegetables. My mom canned lots of fruits and vegetables for winter. We had a root cellar that kept carrots, turnips, parsnips, potatoes, onions and cabbage all winter long. We cut ice off the reservoir and stored it in sawdust in an insulated icehouse. In the summer we would put blocks of ice in the ice box to keep things cold. We could have ice to make ice cream on the holidays with the old crank ice cream freezer. We made our own bread, biscuits, rolls, cookies, pies, cakes and cobblers from scratch. If we forgot when we started the last loaf of bread, we could have a special treat of fried "Baptist bread." We purposely forgot sometimes.

I started milking cows when I was ten years old and didn't stop until I went to college. For 365 days a year, from four in the morning to four in the afternoon, I was in the milk barn. During World War II, my dad and I milked forty-five cows and hauled the milk to the Army

Base fifty miles away every day. We finally got electricity after the war through the Rural Electrification Administration; our place was the first to turn on lights and we also got milking machines. Glory be, no more milking by hand!

I went to a one-room elementary school and never had anyone in my class. I was then sent to town school with two other students. There were thirteen of us in my high school class and I graduated valedictorian. It is strange how disconnected I got when I went away to college. I had been a muscled, sunburned farm worker. I arrived in my sister's hand-me-downs. I had never done laundry or cooked a meal. Suddenly, I was supposed to be a lady, still working, but now cleaning house, baby-sitting and serving food in the dormitory, as well as making good grades. In college, I wanted to be an engineer because I loved airplanes and had made models for years. Unfortunately, I failed so many hours I could not even transfer out of the department. The counseling office tested me and decided I would be best suited to go into Physical Education.

As I look back at those years from 1949 to 1959, it was pretty much just play, study, date, make friends, buy cars and move from Colorado to California to Alabama to Texas to California to Indiana. At the age of 28, I arrived in Indiana for my first teaching job at the Medical Center. I decided that if I liked it, I just might settle down, get married and raise a family; I did like it, and had a daughter and son, and I now have four grandchildren.

I feel my professional life has been very successful. Since I had polio when I was fourteen, I received a lot of physical therapy. Before I graduated, three of my professors started talking to me about going into physical therapy — so I did. What a blessing to know that two weeks into the program I had found what I wanted to do with my life. I received my education through the Air Force. After the Air Force, I went back and got my Master's degree so I could teach physical therapy. I spent forty years looking for easier, better and faster ways to help the body do what it needed to do; working with children has made it much more fun. I am now retired from a one-on-one, hands-on, private pediatric practice that I had sustained for over thirty years. I taught at the university for twelve years, wrote a textbook and a book for parents, and taught workshops on the local, state, national and international level for forty years. I still love to teach, to turn people on to learning, to see the light dawn in their eyes.

In 1983, my son and I moved to Idaho for him to start high school and for us to change our lifestyle. We wanted out of the fast lane with all the drive and competition. We came to Idaho and felt as though we had stepped back in time ten or twenty years to a much slower pace, to a place where people told the truth and had lives outside their jobs, with time to camp, hunt, hike, fish, boat and just enjoy life.

Even with all the long hours and hard work, I remember my childhood as a good time. I loved the earth, the smell of the plowed ground, the new mown hay, the birds singing, the water running in the creeks, going fishing, being out in the sun, watching the clouds, and having the wind in my face. I belonged to the earth and she sustained us even through the worst of times. I think of all the things I thought were so important: honesty, integrity, pride in a job well done, punctuality, tolerance, compassion, commitment, love, support, fun, and the ability to laugh at yourself. Of course,

having been raised to solve problems, to be independent, to be resourceful and to know that I could do anything I set my mind to made me a very strong professional. I would not change one single thing in my life because living and learning and growing is a journey; it is a process, not a destination. We earn the privilege of living each day and surrender it as one full lifetime in preparation for the next day, should we be fortunate enough to awaken. I hope I can be this example to my children, my grandchildren and every individual I meet.

Mari Carmen Egurrola Totorica

"It was my proudest day, becoming an American citizen."

Carmen is preparing rice pudding in her kitchen to feed her hungry grandchildren. "I love to cook and my family appreciates this." Famous for her delicious Basque cuisine, she is featured along with her recipes in *Sunset Magazine,* the May 2000 edition. Representatives from the magazine spent a day in her home while she prepared Basque food and then they sampled appealing platefuls of what was filling her kitchen with an enticing aroma. Perhaps one of the reasons she fixes rice pudding frequently is because she recalls how delicious the plain rice tasted to her when she was just five years old. She and her family had survived the bombing of Guernica that demolished their home during the Spanish Civil War (1936-39). The first food she ate as a war refugee was rice and bread and "It was so delicious."

Her father was working at his post office job when her family heard the roar of German planes. Residents dashed for cover as her mother ran up a hill and huddled beneath trees with her children. She warned them to hide, be still and pray. Afterwards, they walked through the thick, black smoke and dust, fearful of what they would discover. Along the way, her mother told them not to look, anxious to protect them from unspeakable sights. Their father found them two hours later and they felt profound relief that they were all safe. Mom said, "We don't have a home but we're all okay." They stayed with relatives until her father earned enough money to rebuild their lives. Some nights, the visions returned and Carmen raced with pounding feet and heart to a familiar spot where shadows from overhead never leave.

Meanwhile, in Idaho, another Basque mother told her son, "You are going to be a bachelor and should go back to the Basque country and meet women." Carmen met Ted, her husband-to-be, while working in a hotel in Guernica. She was waiting tables and then one customer asked if she would go out with him. Carmen and Ted married in Guernica and moved to the United States in 1952. Ted worked for the State Highway Department in Boise, Idaho.

Carmen had left her family and everyone she'd known in Spain. "This was a difficult time for me, because I didn't speak the language and I missed talking to people. I was so happy to find a radio station with Nat King Cole singing songs in Spanish. Having our own house and a garden with flowers was like being rich! There was no one living above us and when I went outside, no clothes overhead dripped on me. In Spain, we had no cars, washers or dryers, so I was glad for all the amenities in this country. Appreciate what you have because not everyone has what you have.

"The first job I took before our children were born didn't work out because I couldn't communicate. There was an ad in the newspaper for a housekeeper and caregiver for a couple's children. When I applied for this job, I was told they wanted a Basque woman because they heard we are hard workers. I worked for almost a year before our children were born: Dolores, Tony, Maria Carmen, Rosa Maria, Gloria, Ted, Teresa and Miguel, who was stillborn. I was fortunate that I didn't have to work outside the home so I could stay with my children. When our children wanted to spend the night with other kids I just didn't understand this. I thought they should sleep, play and eat in their own home and not run around the neighborhood.

"I took English classes. It took me five years to become a U.S. citizen and the day I accomplished this was my proudest day. Then I learned to drive and I could go places.

"I love to sing and one day someone said to me, 'Carmen, I know you can teach singing,' and these words gave me the confidence I needed. I have taught Basque songs to children of all cultures for 22 years at the Basque Center. I've taught 180 children at one time. When I am out some place and my students spot me and say, 'There's my teacher,' I feel so good. I organized the Boise Basque Choir with the help of my son. It began with seven voices (including my alto) and now has fifty members. We sing for weddings and other occasions, have sung in the Morrison Center and for other community events. How I love music!

"I enjoy the Basque Center, where I visit with friends and play *briska* (a game similar to bridge), and enjoy watching *jota* (lively danc-

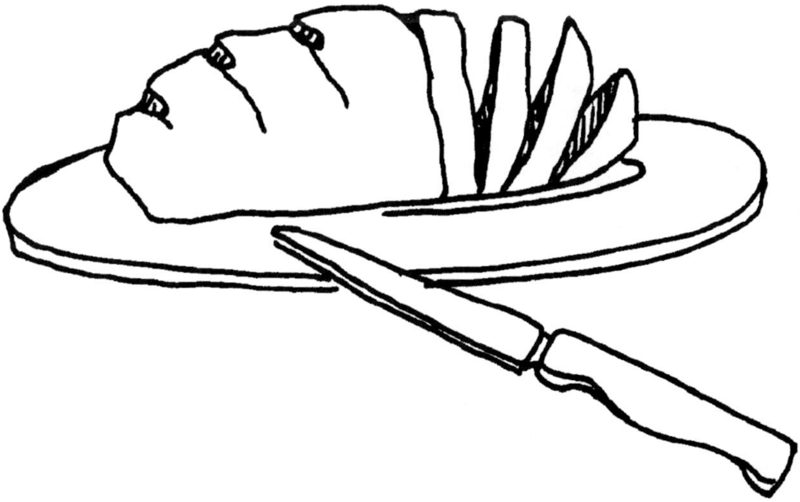

ing). The Sheepherders' Ball is a popular event too. My regular day to go to the Basque Center is Sunday. I have served on the Board of Directors, earning the position of president of the Center. This office helped me understand city laws and to learn about people. I am the Basque Center community organizer and my family helps me with this. I go to the YMCA and I love to garden and every plant in my yard is growing there because I planted it. I learned to swim 21 years ago and I feel good about that. I almost drowned during my first lesson."

Carmen is the eldest of six siblings and her mother and relatives live in the Basque country of Spain. Carmen has traveled to Spain fifteen times; her mother has visited in Boise twice and she is fifteen times a great-grandmother.

Adelaide Woodcook

"I couldn't do any more than fail."

We were newlyweds of only one week; I was wearing my going-away outfit and my handsome husband his only dark suit. The flashing light at the crossroads gave importance to our mission as we swayed gently in the train that carried us to our first pastorate. We alighted at our assigned destination. I checked the seams in my first pair of nylons before walking the five blocks along Main Street, luggage in hand, to the little white church and our first home — five rooms off the back of the sanctuary platform. It was 1942 and I was twenty-one years old.

This was my dream — the only possible role I could fill. I had been raised in a radically religious home, confined by walls of fear and quiet. The outside world was threatening and foreign to me. At the end of my two years at church college, my parents were glad to transfer me into the arms of a graduated minister. Being the wife of a minister let me live in my comfort zone.

Even though I was crippled socially and emotionally, I was fortunate to have an outgoing personality and innate talent. I threw myself into the work of the church for thirty-four years. I played the piano, directed musical programs and pageants, and taught classes of up to 300 people, besides entertaining guests and raising my two children. My husband was highly motivated and successful and at the end of our ministry we were pastoring the third largest church in our denomination. His success was my only reward.

During our third pastorate, I began to experience an inner awakening. I longed for some fulfillment of my own, some life outside my confined world that would give me personal worth and value. I was living out my parents' rigid directives rather than being true to myself.

My first step into the outer world came while living in a university town. I began to dream of going back to school and finishing my undergraduate degree. I was almost forty years old when I walked into the awesome administration building (with my twenty-year-old transcript) and registered for my first classes. I couldn't do any more than fail. Six years later, in 1966, I had a Master's degree in Elementary Education, as well as a high GPA and three years of teaching experience to my credit. However, I learned far more than academics. I was exposed to relationships with people outside my small world. I began to see myself as intelligent and capable as I gradually risked my own inner charity.

Then came a new pastorate and a phone call that again changed my life. The dean of our denominational college wanted to interview me for a teaching position. I was stunned. Surely there must be a mistake. However, when classes resumed in the fall of 1967, I was a member of the faculty, teaching and supervising student teachers in the Education Department. Listening to my own inner voice had given me an exciting career of my own, which I enjoyed for fifteen years, at last retiring with a Citation of Excellence in Teaching.

During these years of teaching and retirement, I held retreats and seminars on the value of self-worth, joyfully sharing what I was learning. Later, I developed seminars on "Living From Within," which taught that each of us has a divine spirit and purpose for being on the planet. This divinity in us can lead to inner peace and fulfillment if we are willing to be scrupulously honest with ourselves and trust our inner voice for guidance.

Down through the years I learned this process by becoming aware of my feelings, which stem from the real person inside. These feelings let me know who that person is. It is then that I can admit my shadow side and find an honesty and integrity that gives me freedom to move closer toward the person my Creator meant me to be. This commitment to keep faith with one's self may have its price in terms of relationships — friends and family who may not understand and to whom you may present a challenge.

My increasing independence was difficult for my husband and added stress to an already unhappy marriage. At the time of my retirement, we had a beautiful lakeside home on three acres where we enjoyed our riding horses, visits from our five grandchildren, and family celebrations. It was all picture perfect but I could pretend no longer. I was almost seventy years old when I divorced my husband of forty-seven years.

Today, I am almost eighty years old, have a beautiful townhouse and am more than financially comfortable — an outward appreciation of inner harmony. Best of all, my life is full of loving family and friends, as well as unspeakable love, joy and peace inside myself. It's never too late to begin this exciting journey.

Mary Daley

"Learning never ends."

My life has been shaped, as is everyone's, by experiences and choices. Life is a great adventure with many hills and valleys, and with constant challenges for learning and improving one's self and one's community.

I grew up in Lincoln, Nebraska, the fourth of five children in a blue-collar family. We lived on the edge of town. Trees and fields of sunflowers were my playground. I read many a book sitting in the highest crotch of any nearby tree.

At the age of ten, when new homes were being built in my sunflower playground, I turned to baby-sitting. My first job was playing with several children under the age of six for a couple of hours one or two mornings a week. Each family paid me a quarter. Soon I was baby-sitting in the evenings at thirty-five cents an hour. My working life had begun.

I got a work permit when I was fourteen and I started bussing tables at the YWCA cafeteria, serving banquets at a downtown hotel, and clerking in a clothing store. I didn't want to be a nurse or a teacher — the only careers I felt were open to me — so I took secretarial classes. I was a part-time legal secretary my last two years of high school. Through college, I worked at a mail-advertising firm as a secretary and analyst.

That's where I experienced my first sex discrimination: the guys made more per hour doing the same work I did and were allowed to smoke at their desks. I could only smoke in the break room. I had one advantage: state law prohibited me from working more than 54 hours per week. I remember one hectic summer week when my hours were in by Wednesday midnight. I had the rest of the week off.

The University of Nebraska was great. I joined numerous organizations, served on many boards and committees, and attended events that I came to appreciate later even more than I did at the time. As a Speech and English major, I attended Broadway shows put on by road companies and every university theater production. I was at the Homecoming Dance the year Duke Ellington played. I was at every Nebraska football game and most basketball games.

Two weeks after graduation in 1961, I married an Idaho man and moved to Sun Valley for the summer. Then we moved to Moscow, Idaho, where my husband earned a law degree and his Master's in accounting. I worked for two years in the university business office, then stayed home and raised three kids. In 1966, we moved to Boise and had three more kids. I was a homemaker for 14 years.

When I returned to outside work, I did temporary jobs for six months. This led to secretarial work at the Idaho Migrant Council for three years, and the Idaho Human Rights Commission for twelve years. My interest in human rights took a giant leap when I worked for the Northwest Coalition Against Malicious Harassment for five years, covering the state of Idaho and helping communities to accept diversity and stand against organized hatred. Lack of funding forced my departure from that job and I began work for the Idaho Youth Ranch in development and fundraising.

Along the way, many things happened. Alcoholism and its devastating effects on a family entered the picture. After twenty-one years of marriage, my husband and I divorced. I spent eight years in Al-Anon activities, learning, internalizing, meditating and changing. It was painful, but time well spent. My entire extended family is emotionally healthier thanks to the twelve step program.

My most noteworthy accomplishment began in 1985. The Idaho Human Rights Commission and Boise State University sponsored the first Peaceful Settlements Conference, bringing 500 people together to learn about and discuss mediation. I was attracted to community mediation like a magnet.

A group of people began meeting to develop something similar to Community Boards of Boise. One group went to San Francisco to learn organizing; I was in a second group that learned to teach community mediation. My administrative skills helped form an organization called The Sounding Board. I was the first president and attended my first National Conference on Peacemaking and Conflict Resolution in Denver in 1986. I later attended conferences in North Carolina and Oregon.

Much more importantly, while I was active in the organization, we taught community mediation to over 500 people in the Treasure Valley and many more after that until The Sounding Board was dissolved and re-developed at Boise State University. I helped train and write grants, I sat on panels and coordinated volunteers, I did case development and much of the administrative work for the first three years. We resolved many, many disputes in neighborhoods for ten years.

I was also on the board and helped with the secretarial/clerical work of the Idaho Mediation Association, a statewide umbrella organization for anyone interested in mediation. When the Sounding Board was dissolved after ten years, some of its assets were given to the I.M.A. to set up an office, which is still in my home (with paid part-time staff).

Mediation taught me many new and useful skills: active listening, conflict resolution, negotiation and arbitration. It taught me how to live with, work with, and help my fellow human beings. As I taught these skills to people of all ages from all walks of life, I learned again how great it is to love and appreciate all people. Material things pale fast in comparison to watching someone learn to really listen and actively resolve issues with a neighbor or family member. That's what it's all about. My mother taught me well: learning never ends. My mission in life is to leave the world a little better than I found it.

Bethine Church

"Just living is dangerous but, if you try, life can be truly rewarding."

My father was lawyer, Mayor, legislator, Governor and U.S. Federal District Judge in Idaho. I campaigned for him early in my life, asking a shoe clerk if he would "boat" for my Daddy, though I didn't know what a "boat" was. Pop twinkled telling wonderful stories, but he also spoke of the serious things in life — children who couldn't go to school because they had no shoes during the Depression. At the dinner table, we never had the kind of conversation of those times. We talked about all the taboo subjects: law cases, religion and politics. The only subject shunned seemed to be sex. However before his time, Pop treated me, though a girl, like I was capable of sound thought. I was expected to have ideas and to argue if I had a different point of view. He understood the abilities of women from the very first.

This placed me in good stead for after coming to Boise, all of my debate friends, including Frank Church, came to the house Sunday evenings to raid the fridge and talk public affairs. We also talked about the situation in Europe, for this was in 1940. Then came the war. Frank enlisted, was in the China, Burma and India Theater, and returned to finish undergraduate schooling at Stanford. In 1947, he married me on the front porch of our ranch in the Salmon River Mountains. I simply buckled my seatbelt and knew that life would never be peaceful but it certainly would never be boring.

When I was a teenager, I decided I would never a marry a lawyer or politician, but at the moment Frank said if we could raise the money, he would run for the Democratic Senate seat, I knew at last that the political spoon in my mouth had made me like the prizefighter hearing the bell! We sold the house, moved our child and our base in with my folks and used what we had to run on. I knew how much it meant to Frank, and I knew how much it meant to me.

Besides a political background, my family gave me one other special preparedness for my partnership with Frank's life. My dad said, "Arrange things for your family in the best way possible, then go with him — one day your family will be grown. And then you and Frank will be close if you've known what he cared about, what were the hurts, what were the triumphs. After all, you can slip at home in the bathtub and never have lived at all. Just living is dangerous but often, if you try, life can be truly rewarding."

The first campaign was truly fun, for we had no position at stake, just a lifetime ahead to recoup. In those days, money raising wasn't such a big thing; I held the boom mike for our television spots. It felt as though everything we did was absolutely the most individual and intensive campaigning that anyone had ever done.

When we went to the Senate, Frank and I bought a house just across the district line in Maryland. I remember one winter when a big snowstorm raged for two days. Late on the second afternoon, I put on my boots and babushka and headed out. There were seven houses on our street and I knocked and was received by each home as though I was a person from Mars. My mission was to invite everyone to our house for a potluck. It was awkward at first, but it turned out to be a really good party. All my neighbors became good friends.

Like others, I led two lives — one with my feet still in Idaho, one in the linguistic fields of Washington life, and all the time trying to balance a growing nine-year-old and a baby. I kept a house in Idaho and Maryland, every two years after the local state campaigns, replacing broken down equipment and doing the major painting and necessary repair work. The carpet was due for replacement when we ran for President in 1976; we'd run out of throw rugs to cover the bare spots.

Many wives don't like political life at all and, while liking their husbands, plan a life of their own completely away from the political field. Some find fulfillment in homemaking, community roles or careers of their own. As in real life, politics has its triumphs and tragedies. The only difference seems to be the growing, glaring spotlight that has been focused on the wife and family part of the political scene. I love to cook and when I was really mad at the Administration (Democrat or Republican), I'd cook gourmet meals to get rid of the frustration. I've never really lost the weight. My only advice to new wives is to be themselves and do it their own way. If one feels a sense of coming unglued with the pressure, one can take a choice: yelling a lot or jogging. I would also like to mention that I have real sympathy for the check-bouncers, because my first four checks written in Idaho after Frank became Senator bounced.

During Frank's years in the Senate, I felt we'd fought through the battle for statehood for Hawaii and Alaska, and we flew in a bush plane almost into the slopes of Mt. McKinley, to see that great mountain in the heart of a brand new state. Two years after the election of President Kennedy, we went to all the places our troops were stationed in the Far East. We went up to the DMZ in Korea on a snowy Thanksgiving Day, where we met a group of terribly young Idaho soldiers stationed at this barren front on the world. We flew in a helicopter out of Saigon, Vietnam, to a fortified village, looking out past the young corporal with a knife in his belt, a pistol on his hip and his machine gun with bullets in the clip. In 1976, Frank was invited to be the keynote speaker at the Brussels Conference on Soviet Jewry. But aside from the wonderful experiences of coming to know some of the world a bit more intimately, the world of official Washington was a brave new place for me too.

My life might have been easier, more routine, but the truth of the matter is that I'm thankful for just the experiences I've described, as well as for the people of Idaho and the nation that I met campaigning. It's truly been a Cinderella experience. It was especially strange to be changing diapers and struggling to get a baby-sitter, then putting on a long dress and meeting exceptional people like Adlai Stevenson and Charles DeGaulle. My life has been helped by flexible children and wonderful friends, both here in Idaho and in Washington, and a father who loved politics and people and taught me to feel the same way, and a mother who figured that anyone could learn to do anything they had to do. My return to Idaho has rounded out the circle. You can go home again if it was truly home — and Idaho is!

One of my greatest sorrows when Frank died was the fact that we enjoyed being together so much that we could have had fun getting old together. As it is, I'm now incredibly busy in my new life being on the Governor's Home Health Care Task Force and working with the Frank Church Chair of Public Affairs and other community projects and boards. Though I've never held a real job, I've felt that I had a full time one when Frank was alive and sometimes I feel now more like a PR firm than his widow. In other words, I couldn't have spent life more liberated or with one more job.

Jayne Jones

"I got to keep moving because at my age, to 'stop' takes on a whole new meaning."

I'm always ready for a new adventure. Throughout my life I have been attracted to the elements of danger and speed. Whether it was driving cars, flying airplanes, skiing, tai chi, horseback riding, education or relationships, I have embraced the thrill of the great adventure. Of course, I have broken almost every major bone in my body. But I take responsibility for the injuries and usually got over the mishaps rapidly.

Skiing has always been the central thrill of my life. I skied until I was eighty-seven years old. My sons sped up the decision for me to stop skiing by mysteriously helping my skis to disappear from the garage. But even though skiing is no longer a part of my winter days, I do believe in the importance of exercise, so I walk and do tai chi on a regular basis.

I come from an old Mormon family. I remember my grandfather telling me that one of his wives wouldn't get out of the wagon until he built her a home. I understand that a house was built right away. Women were always admired and respected in my family, and children were seen as gifts from God and treated fairly. I never felt discrimination. I acquired this from my mother who was quite liberated and had her own voice.

My father owned the Utah Woolen Mills and was quite successful. It was located in Salt Lake City and employed sixty men. Father went to Philadelphia each year to buy the latest knitting machines and had a Syrian mechanic who kept them running. The Woolen Mills produced all types of blankets, woolen underwear, and woolen knitted petticoats. It was my job to crochet the armholes and bottoms of the woolen petticoats. I remember many days walking to Daddy's work and sitting for hours in his office. I enjoyed being around the business. Housekeeping and cooking were those things that my three sisters enjoyed, but not me, not even to this day.

I went to the University of Utah and received a degree in Business Law and Language. The two instructors who I remember most vividly are Vardis Fisher, who was my composition instructor, and later on, Wallace Stegner. These educators believed in me and encouraged me to continue my journey toward independence and liberation.

I love to fly so years after those college days and no one was surprised when I mentioned that I was taking flying lessons. I was one of Idaho's first woman pilots. No knitting socks and folding bandages for me during the war. Instead, I became a licensed pilot so that I might teach students from the College of Idaho how to fly. But about the time I received my license, the war ended so I never pursued my teaching aspiration. I co-owned three planes and loved every minute spent soaring through the vast open air. I continued flying for many years. My children worried about the dangers as I got older but this toy was much too big to mysteriously disappear like the skis.

After college, in 1931, I married Leon C. Jones who was a kind, gentle and considerate soul mate. Within a few years after marrying we had five children, Leon Lloyd, Rock Hubbard, Donnette McAdams, Michael Robert and Timothy Boston. Leon was immersed in financial business enterprises and so was I. After we had been married for ten years, I became the state president of the American Association of University Women (AAUW) and worked with the League of Women Voters. I raised my five wonderful children while supporting my husband's demanding schedule (at the Simplot Company) and pursuing my own interests. So I was a very busy young woman.

My husband died in 1978. After his death I was in a black hole. My friend Barry Stevens gave me the book written by Chung-Liang "Al" Huang, *Embrace Tiger Return To Mountain.* Chung is a *tai chi* master. The book appealed to my dangerous side, which was transforming into something mysterious and exotic. I wanted the invisible to become visible in my life. After twenty plus years, it continues to be a great component of my life. I see each day as a new and unique experience. I am able to embrace the moment with new and exciting vitality. Every day upon rising, I see potential in myself. All of my life I have been free to dance, sing, move, muse and enjoy nature. With all of life's instabilities, these feelings are a gift.

A substantial change that is needed now is for society to create a new life style. *Things* seem to be much too important. Collecting all the junk has to stop. We need to simplify. We need to balance patience and forgiveness to make this world a better place. And as I consider the road marks in a life well lived, ninety years worth, I believe that forgiveness is the most important force to exert on anyone.

I feel that it is crucial to stay neat and orderly in yourself and in your surroundings. By maintaining order and tidiness, we are showing respect to ourselves and earning respect from others.

I will become the young age of ninety-one before the year 2000 is over. I have hit a few bumps along the way but the ride has been one of beauty and education. I have seen the sights, I have smelled the fragrant aroma of success and I have tasted the bittersweet challenge of grief and fallibility. But I have not given up or given in to the word failure.

Carmalita Zamzow

"With all that I have gone through in my one hundred and three years, the most important area of my life has been raising my children. Family and faith has always sustained me and made me whole."

I was born in Edina, Missouri, in 1897, the eldest of nine children. After several years of drought in Missouri, my family packed and moved to Boise in 1902. We came by train. I was five years old and remember that the trip took five days and four nights. We settled in Boise's North End on 19th and Hazel Streets. My father took a job with Foster's Brickyard near what is now Camel's Back Park. Just about everyone in the North End, including us, kept a cow staked out by the house. All of us kids had chores we had to do to keep the home running. One of mine was taking my dad his lunch in an old metal lunch bucket every day. I remember watching big ore wagons with massive wheels rumble down Harrison Boulevard.

In 1905, we moved to an eighty-acre farm in Meridian. As the oldest child, much of my childhood was spent helping my mother raise my five brothers and three sisters, cleaning house, washing, mending and baking. Just about everything we ate came from the farm, and all our meals were cooked from scratch. My jobs included churning butter, making soap from rendered lard, and making yeast from hops. There was no refrigeration, so we kept our food cool in a dirt cellar under the house. Animals were butchered in the winter so the meat could be hung up to freeze.

Although we were largely self-sufficient, everyone understood the importance of neighbors. It was the rule that neighbors helped one another out. If a neighbor had a new baby or an illness, I was sent to help. I remember when I was twelve years old being sent into the homes of people I had never met to spend several days helping with a newborn baby or sick child.

I went to school at Meridian, a three-mile walk from our house. Education wasn't considered important for girls, it was more important that they learn to maintain a home and raise a family. My formal education ended after I finished the eighth grade so I could spend more time helping at home with the chores and raising the younger children. Religion was a very important part of my family. Every Sunday we rode the ten miles to St. John's Cathedral in my dad's wagon. It had a canvas-covered top and was pulled by a team of workhorses. In the winter, Dad would heat lava rocks in the oven and wrap them in cloth to keep us warm for the trip.

I met August Zamzow in 1913, while I was working as a waitress at Beams Bakery. We were married in 1915 when I was 17 years old. (Seventeen was not especially young for a girl to marry in those days.)

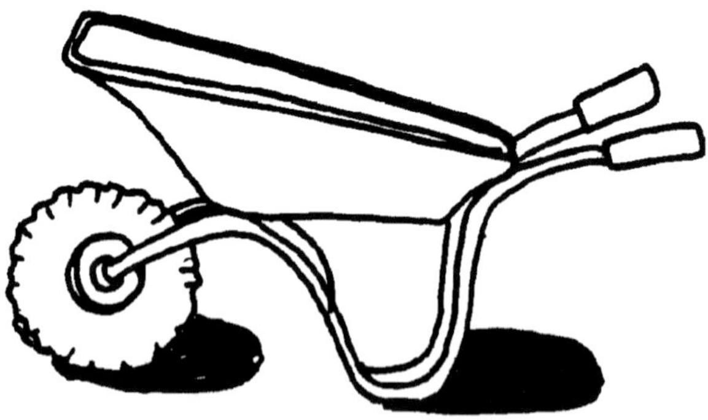

My husband and I moved to a farm in the Star area where my first child was born in 1916. In those days, keeping a home was a full-time job. I canned our fruit, vegetables and meat. I sewed our clothes, milked cows, fed the farm hands and cared for my family. Our entertainment was dancing and having picnics with friends and neighbors. We formed the Blue Valley Dance Club and held weekly dances in neighbors' homes.

By the time World War I started, I was pregnant with my second child. I feared my husband would be called away to fight, leaving me with two small children and a farm to take care of. However, he was exempted from military service because we were in the process of growing many acres of wheat, considered essential for the war effort.

In 1918, I lost my two-month old baby to a strain of influenza that killed many people around the world, including hundreds of soldiers. My husband and I also became ill with the flu. Then I contracted pneumonia and was given the last rites. I was not expected to survive, but I did.

Our family grew to five children and in 1928 we moved to a forty-acre farm on Cole Road. We worked hard to make a living but there never seemed to be any extra money. When the Depression hit, it didn't change our lives significantly. We continued to grow our own food and make most of what we needed to get by. So though we were poor by today's standards, we didn't feel poor. We always had food on the table and didn't suffer the way many others in America did at the time.

It became more and more difficult to provide for a family of five by farming, and the long hours of heavy work began to take a toll on my husband's health. Finally, his doctor recommended that he get into a different line of work. In 1935, he bought a mill on Fairview Avenue and named it "Zamzow's Coal and Feed." This was a big step for us.

Our lives had been tied to the land and it had always provided us what we needed. Now we were going into a business. Our living would depend upon our ability to sell to our customers.

After we bought the mill, my daily work became even harder. In addition to the jobs of homemaking and raising children, I had to help my husband run the store. I would finish my chores in the morning and then walk the two and a half miles to help out at the store. We had a car but my husband did the driving. I never learned to drive. I kept the store clean and made displays. In addition to animal feed, we sold coal for stoves and furnaces, weighed and bought grain and hay from farmers in the valley, and pumped gas by hand for automobiles. I was raising five kids and also worked as the handyman at the store. I did whatever needed to be done, and supervised our kids who were also required to help out in their spare time. At the age of 38, I was a very busy woman.

By 1936, our business was successful enough that we were able to buy a new home on Fairview Avenue only about a half-mile from the store. It was exciting for me because this was my first home with running water and indoor plumbing. Although there were only three bedrooms and one bathroom for the seven of us, we were blessed with a very nice home. And because our grown sons had now taken an active role in the business, I was able to stay home much more.

But that didn't last very long. World War II started and both my sons and a son-in-law left for military service. Once again, I had to resume my spot as the store's general handyman. When my sons returned from the war, my husband and I decided it was time to retire. We arranged for our sons to take over the business and spent many wonderful years together without the stress of business between us.

My husband August died in 1978. There are now eight Zamzow's stores, and they are owned and managed by the generation of Zamzows. I feel great pride when I think back to that first store on Fairview Avenue where my husband and I worked as a team to meet the challenges of a new career. We never dreamed that we were starting a business that would continue to prosper and grow and remain a part of our family for the next 65 years.

I feel my life has been a pioneering one made up of hard work, difficult times and much joy. I am happy to have lived through and experienced the many changes in the world from 1897 to 2000. I am looking forward to new experiences in the future. In reflecting back, the most important thing in my life has been my children. Family and faith have always sustained me and made me whole.

The past is only the present become invisible
and mute; and because it is invisible and mute,
its memoried glances and its murmurs
are infinitely precious. We are tomorrow's past.

— Mary Webb

Maxine Freeman

"'Maxine, you really must come to the party,
we need some OLDER women.'
I was twenty-eight."

When working for First Federal Savings of Chicago, I had the exalted title of savings teller supervisor. It was my job to schedule those who would work the half-day on Saturdays. Tellers who were scheduled for those Saturdays were expected to be there unless they were sick enough to be in the hospital. Failure to attend to Saturday duties under any other circumstances was to be subject to some disciplinary action. Before the teller was scheduled on the Saturday she was always given a day off from the preceding week. This was the compensation for working on a Saturday.

On this particular Saturday, one of the bright young ladies called in sick, and I had to work a cash drawer to cover her position. When I arrived home that evening after work, the phone rang. It was Alice inviting me to a "mixer" party that evening. I blurted out, "But Alice, you are ill. Certainly too ill for a party."

Her casual response was, "Oh, no, I wasn't ill, just hung-over."

I was furious. This was a possible firing offense, a disciplinary note in the file at the very least. And besides, it was I who had to cover her shift.

While I continued to be at a loss for words, Alice launched into reasons why I should come to the party. What makes this tale a tale is the topper: "Maxine, you really must come to the party," she said, "we need some OLDER women." I was twenty-eight.

The tale could easily end there or continue.

I was so nonplused I went to the party. I just couldn't believe that Alice had admitted to me that she did not come to work for such an excuse and that she had called me an OLDER woman.

The tale could easily end there or continue.

There was quite a group of unattached, attractive people at the party. We began various friendships and after a few months, when three of the guys rented a house together, they threw a party. I was included on the guest list. Every time I turned around at that party, John Freeman was close by.

We have been married for forty-two years.

The tale could easily end there and it does.

Helen Thomson

"Those were the good old days."

My generation witnessed an incredible number of inventions and developments, which now are taken for granted. The zipper, for instance, replaced buttons on men's trousers and women's clothing. Nylons replaced the silk hosiery, which took forever to dry.

The first radios were crystal sets. I heard my first broadcast wearing headphones. The mob scene was being described in Chicago at the funeral of silent motion picture star Rudolph Valentino.

Movie fans flocked to see the first talking picture, *The Jazz Singer,* starring Al Jolson singing "Sonny Boy." Some time later, color was added to the movie screen.

When I was a child, our food was kept cool in a big square icebox. A card placed in our front window indicated how much ice was needed for the day. The iceman used tongs to deliver the big block of ice slung over his shoulder. The ice melted into a pan underneath the icebox which had to be emptied frequently.

I saw my first airplane, a fragile looking aircraft, in a field just outside our small town. Everyone rushed out to see the little open cockpit plane. And those who were brave enough (and had the funds to pay the pilot) could have a brief flight over the town.

The first television sets were expensive and only two households in our neighborhood had them. But all the children were welcome to watch their favorite shows after school.

My generation grew up and worked during the Depression. I have had to survive the wars so I know how precious and short life is. During this time there was no social security, food stamps, or welfare programs for widows and dependent children. So when my father died in September 1922, my mother was left with two small children and without the skills needed to make a living in the small town of Plainfield, Indiana, just outside of Indianapolis.

We survived that first winter with the help of the Ku Klux Klan. At that time, the KKK was not considered a racist hate group but just another club or lodge. I remember Mother telling us that we were going to have company but not to be afraid when the company arrived at the door. When there was a knock mother opened it. On the porch stood a group of masked, white- hooded visitors who walked silently into the room bearing big baskets of food and a few wrapped Christmas presents. They continued bringing food for several months without ever muttering a word. When mother would open the door, the masked men would walk in, put the baskets of food on the table, nod to each of us and leave.

In the spring, we moved in Indianapolis where my mother became an early career woman. I was fortunate to attend a high school where office training was offered as well as college preparatory classes. Although I wanted to go to college, there was no money for my education. But one of my teachers encouraged me, assuring me that I could work my way through college. So I did stenographic work for three years and saved my money.

On the Indiana University campus, there were many job opportunities for at least thirty-five cents per hour. I took dictation from the Dean of the Graduate School, the football coach and Dr. Alfred Kinsey. The thirty-five cents per hour went a long way. It bought the plate lunch at the Book Nook, a popular campus hangout. The Book Nook was where Hoagy Carmichael had composed his famous song, "Star Dust," on the battered piano in the front of the store.

Living in the dormitory cost $35 per month. It was slightly more in the sorority house, but members could wash the dishes after each meal to reduce the monthly cost. (This was long before electric dishwashers.)

I majored in Journalism, which too has changed. We were instructed to be objective and never to insert our own opinions or beliefs. Today, investigative reporting is the norm. And the five W's of journalism, who, what, where, when and why, are either forgotten or ignored.

One of the most interesting and challenging positions I took was with the American Red Cross as public relations director during World War II in Tulsa, Oklahoma. We had hundreds of volunteers rolling bandages, knitting sweaters and making robes and slippers for the service men, and making small bags, which were filled with toiletries for the soldiers as they headed for overseas duty.

I learned that racial prejudice still prevailed in Tulsa when I took a glossy print to the local newspaper editor. The picture showed four service men (one of them African-American) in an overseas hospital wearing the robes that had been made by volunteers. The editor looked at it and handed it back to me.

"You don't expect for me to run that, do you?" he said.

Tulsa was where I met my husband. I had already signed up for an overseas assignment but he vetoed that idea, saying, "One person overseas is enough."

So I stayed home while he was in the Battle of the Bulge in Germany. And my own battle of the bulge was giving birth to our first son while my husband was away. Raising our four children was the best career of all. Now, retirement is the culmination of the long years of working.

On July 18, 2000, I will be eighty-seven years young. I am looking forward to blowing out one hundred candles on my birthday cake. Only thirteen years to go.

Billie Baker

"You don't expect me to stay home, do you?"

My name is Billie Baker. I am eighty-five years young. I am four feet and ten inches tall with snow-white hair and bright red fingernails. I came to Boise fifteen years ago when I decided that I could no longer live alone. I wanted to be near my daughter Donna because she had the most fun. I have joined the fun since arriving.

I joined a church and became quite active in the Rebecca Lodge and the Senior Citizen Center. In fact, last year I met my man (my boyfriend) at the center.

I like to chauffeur friends to the store, the doctor's office and out to lunch. I love to watch figure skating. I go once in a while to skating competitions and shows when they come to Boise. At the shows I like to sit in the front row so I can give the skater comments and jump up and down and go wild. Soon everyone joins the enthusiasm. It's a hoot.

A few years ago, my brother's wife died. My brother suffers from early Alzheimer's and the family hired me to stay with my younger brother so that he would not have to go into a convalescent home.

I celebrated my eightieth birthday in Jamaica with family and friends. Later I had a knee replacement, and six weeks after the surgery I was flying to Texas to spend Christmas with my family. When asked about going, I said, "You don't expect me to stay home do you?" My daughter calls me the "gad-about woman" and I hope I have many more "gad-about" years.

HELEN DAGRES

"Don't say 'no' to me or I'll prove I can do it."

Helen's parents were Greek immigrants: "Dad came first and several years later he sent for my mother. They were married in Pocatello, Idaho." Her father owned a fruit stand on Main Street and gradually ended up with half the block, including a lunch counter and three other buildings. Helen and her family helped with these businesses that were located across from the bus station and near the railroad. Servicemen riding the rails stopped to purchase food and cases of beer that her father provided. Their family did very well during World War II, even with the rationing of staples. Her four brothers and one of two sisters went to war, leaving Helen in charge of the business at age seventeen. This experience helped her become a savvy businessperson.

After graduating from high school, Helen took a beauty school vocational course at the southern branch of the University of Idaho. She didn't enjoy doing hair but she wanted to learn how to do her own. At that time, she had no interest in going into the business.

Helen married Frank Dagres, whom she met at church. When he was a child, he worked in the Garden City Gardens. He owned Frank's

Shoe Store in Boise. They bore a son and two daughters and now have two grandchildren. Helen and Frank realized a need for a Greek Orthodox Church in Boise so they undertook this as their first project. There were countless money-making events and people were generous in helping to see this goal come to life. Saint Constantine Church opened its doors to the community and recently celebrated its 40th anniversary.

"I had another dream and worked hard to make it happen. My husband was less than enthusiastic about my plans to open a beauty salon and didn't encourage me toward that goal. Don't say 'no' to me or I'll prove I can do it. I have to have a challenge or else I'm bored. Frank is cautious in business and was skeptical that I would succeed. I wanted to prove to myself that I could reach the goal I planned and it turned out just as I'd planned with hard work and effort.

"Catherine Anacabe was my catalyst, encouraging my business ventures. I went knocking on doors to find property, the first step toward fulfilling my ambition. When my husband saw that I was serious about starting my own business, he bought the farmland that was where the front of the Cole and Ustick shopping center is today. I owned a beauty shop called The House of Venus and had a massage parlor in the back of the shop. The massage parlor was eventually converted to a health center.

"I joined the Hairdressers' Association and held the office of president from 1963 to 1964. The beauty business thrived and then I added rental apartments to this facility. I tried to run a beauty salon in my home, but this didn't work out. The lovely beauty shop I owned in downtown Boise was called House of Venus #2; the building where my salon was is included in the Idaho Historical Society Registry."

Eventually, as Helen was tiring of the salon business, she received a timely purchase offer, which she gladly accepted.

Well known for her marvelous cooking talents, Helen, along with her committee, spends several months preparing for the Greek Food Festival, making *dolmadoes* — a meat, rice and spice combination that is rolled inside a grape leaf and is highly prized for its palatability.

"All my business didn't leave much time for fun. There was much work to be done. But hard work has its own reward. We have traveled to Greece often. In 1970, we took the children to Greece and met our many relatives for the first time. I do wish I'd taken more time with the children, but there is so much to do when operating businesses. It was hard raising my family, trying to meet their needs while handling the demands of business. The kids have been my life and I want to see them happy and thriving.

"I believe the most important thing is to treat people like you want to be treated and then you will succeed. I never had a formal education; I am self-educated to success."

Helen has business instinct and her intuitive investments all turned to gold. But what mattered most to her was to see her dream a reality and to accomplish this on her own. Helen was named Distinguished Citizen in a 1975 edition of *The Idaho Statesman.*

Never doubt that a small group of thoughtful,
committed citizens can change the world;
indeed, it is the only thing that has.

— Margaret Mead

Major Dale Angers

"Regarding my career in the service of our country, I would do it again. This can be of great assistance in developing your work ethics, discipline and love of our nation."

I was born in Texas City, Texas, on August 4, 1913. I was the second and last child of May Phillips and Charles W. Van Vacter. Helen Ann, my only sibling, was six years my senior. My father was a builder. My family moved from Bonner Springs, Kansas, in 1908. Eight years earlier, Galveston, Texas was devastated by a tidal wave from the Gulf of Mexico. More than five thousand residents were killed and many structures demolished. Businesses failed and people weren't interested in moving there. My father left Texas and went to Oklahoma City looking for work. He moved his family there on November 17, 1915.

I graduated from Central High and spent two years at Christian College (now Columbia College) in Columbia, Missouri. In 1931 it was a private women's college and I spent the years of 1931-1933 there. I had planned to enter Missouri University in 1933 to major in engineering in hopes of joining my father in the construction business but my plans changed in August of 1933 when he committed suicide five days after my 20th birthday. The era of the Depression and his ill health had reduced his finances and a mental depression consumed him.

I made a radical switch from engineering to medicine and enrolled at Oklahoma City University. I received a degree in biology and chemistry and was admitted to Oklahoma University Medical College but finances made it impossible for me to go more than one semester. The University Hospital along with the medical school gave me a one-year internship in medical technology. I trained for the year and took my national boards for certification, which I received in January 1937. I worked in the lab field in Oklahoma City and Dallas from 1937 to 1942.

In 1942, Congress passed a law to form the Women's Army Auxiliary Corps. I applied along with thirty thousand other women for the 440 spaces allowed in the first class of officer training. I was fortunate to be one of the 440 selected. The old cavalry post at Fort Des Moines, Iowa, was the first of five training centers to be put in operation. An all male cadre trained us. Some men were not as delighted as others were.

A new bill would have to be passed by Congress to send women to England, Africa and parts of Europe. The Auxiliary was terminated and the Women's Army Corps was recognized. In September 1942, a few weeks after being commissioned, I was sent to a regiment set up for specialty training of enlisted women. My assignment was dispensary officer for a fourteen-bed dispensary in the Savory Hotel, in downtown Des Moines where the regiment was assigned. I supervised the training of the clerks and nurse's aids.

In May 1943, I was sent to Fort Oglethorpe as administrative officer for four station dispensaries. It was the third WAC Training Center, and there were several thousand women in training. Fort Des Moines was the first to be activated and the last to close. I remained at Oglethorpe until December 1943 when I was sent on an interim assignment to take over a WAC medical detachment whose commander had been transferred. There were 132 women in the detachment at

Valley Forge General hospital, which had 1800 beds. The hospital was at Phoenixville, Pennsylvania.

In 1944, I was assigned as a laboratory officer at McGuire General Hospital, which was in its final weeks of construction. McGuire had a three-thousand-bed capacity and was located on the outskirts of Richmond, Virginia. I was the first lab officer assigned to McGuire. I was assigned as supervisor of the Bacteriology, Hematology, Urinalysis, Transfusion Preparation and Blood Banking sections and was responsible for all equipment and lab supplies. I was the commanding officer for a fifty-woman medical detachment.

In 1945, I was the only laboratory officer certified in the American Society of Clinical Pathology at Crile General Hospital outside of Cleveland, Ohio. At this time the Germans had surrendered and the Japanese were still doing their damage until a surprise atom bomb was dropped on two of their large cities on June 5 and August 7.

The women in the WAAC/WAC had been told that the Army would disband the WAC Corps six months after cessation of hostilities. However, they kept a few who wanted to stay waiting for that action. I left the service in 1946 and returned to Oklahoma City. Two weeks later I was hired to run a lab in a residential medical building.

In 1948, a bill was passed in Congress to allow women to be commissioned into the regular Army. I applied and was placed on active duty as a Reserve Officer until the selection for the two hundred spaces was made. New officers were given Army serial numbers as identification. The Director of the Corps, Mary Halloran (still living), was given #1. The other 199 were given their Army Serial Numbers in order of birth dates. I was #101. The army no longer uses this identification method. They now use social security number identification.

After the war I spent over a year in civilian status before returning to the service in December 1948, when orders came commissioning the first two hundred selects. I was assigned to Camp Pickett Station as the only lab officer.

I was sent to Fort Sill, Oklahoma, Station Hospital in 1949 and remained there as the only lab officer until 1950, when I requested a transfer from the medics to my own branch of service, the Women's Army Corps. I had been detailed to the medical service and not commissioned in their Corps. I was assigned to Fort Lee, Virginia, for orientation and training in Army Administration. Upon completion of a four-month course by the Adjutant Generals' School, I was assigned to the Idaho Military District in Boise, Idaho, as Adjutant and Personnel officer. This headquarters handled reserve officers for training and prepared them for readiness if they were called back into active duty. This district sponsored Reserve Officers Training Corps (ROTC). Boise High School and the University of Idaho had the ROTC programs.

My mother's health was failing so I brought her to live in my small Boise home. Two years later, in 1953, I was assigned to the General Depot at Livorno, Italy.

My husband Walt and I stayed at Fort Dix where he had a training brigade of about 5,000 troops in various schools for training. He went back to Korea in October 1966 and I returned to Boise. My mother died in August 1959 while I was at Fort Meade. Walt returned to the United States in 1967 on our wedding anniversary.

My husband and I have been active in military activities since our retirement.

In retrospect, regarding my career in the service of our country, I would do it again. I loved the uniform and although there was some resentment during the war regarding the Women's Army Corps, I am sure that no one regrets the time spent. It is not for everyone but it can be of great assistance in developing your work ethics, discipline and love of our nation. Those items were developed during my childhood. My parents were highly principled and required responsibility from me at an early age.

What we say and what we do
ultimately comes back to us,
so let us own our responsibility,
place it in our own hands
and carry it with dignity and strength.

— Gloria Anzaldua

LaRue Cheney

"I have never wished to live any of my life over. Each step along the way is a grand new adventure."

I come from a family of eight. My parents are Elmer Stevens Heiner and Leah Moon. I was born in Mesa, Arizona, but I have lived in Heyburn, Idaho, since I was three years old. I am the eldest child. I have three brothers, all in Heyburn, and one sister in Kaysville, Utah. I had twin sisters and one brother who all died in infancy.

I was in elementary school during the Depression. We lived on a farm so we always had something to eat. Sometimes it was only potatoes and milk gravy but I never grew tired of it. We also had chickens and eggs. In the spring, we had wild asparagus and, in the summer, we had vegetables from the garden.

Our wardrobes were limited. I had two dresses, one for school and one for Sunday. I wore the homemade flour sack underwear. I remember mama washing the boy's overalls at night and hanging them behind the stove to dry.

Sometimes we had a dime for the Saturday matinee if we wanted to walk to town to see the show. It was only two miles away. We also spent our free time playing outdoor games. The neighborhood was full of children's laughter.

I had planned to go to college to become a speech and English teacher but the big money to be made from the war effort made the choice difficult. I never made it to school. Instead, I worked at Hill Field in Ogden, Utah. My job was issuing tools from the tool crib to the airplane mechanics as they worked on the aircraft. Then the war ended and I returned home.

I suppose that the biggest difference that the war made in my life was the soldier I didn't marry and the Marine I did. The soldier was short, Italian, and very Catholic. I was Mormon. The Marine was tall, handsome, from my hometown, and Mormon. I made the right choice in marriage, not only for myself but also for my children.

I married Harlow Frank Cheney on February 5, 1947. We have four children: Pati Reid of Salt Lake City; Frank, who also lives in Salt Lake; Sally, a paraplegic who lives with us; and Melanie Metzger, who lives in Boise. I have six beautiful grandchildren. So the house is full on the holidays.

Sally was injured in a motorcycle accident in 1973 when she was twenty years old. She had just finished her sophomore year at Brigham Young University and was returning home when she was hit. Some difficult times followed for all of us, especially for Sally. But she has made a wonderful life for herself and is an inspiration to all who know her.

After marriage, I worked as a drug store soda jerk. I made great milkshakes. Then I worked for the Credit Bureau of Burley. I didn't know how much I disliked working with figures until I got into the credit field. What I disliked the most was hounding people for money. I would much rather write about their accomplishments and publish it for all to read. That's where my interest in being a newspaper editor began.

I quit at the credit bureau and took a job as editor of the Heyburnian High School newspaper. I then began sending neighborhood items to the weekly *Minidoka County Newspaper.* I covered the Hopewell area and had about a hundred numbers I called each week.

I did not have a telephone so I would walk to the neighbor's with my two children and use her party line. I would ring an operator and tell her that I was collecting news. She would ring the numbers I gave and when the party answered, I would ask, "Any news today?" The highlights of the news would usually be stories of children visiting from the big city of Boise or Salt Lake City, or someone holding a dinner party or going on a trip.

Then came that memorable day August 1, 1968, when Walt Schramm called me into his office and asked if I was interested in being society editor for a new paper they were starting in Burley, *The Reminder Morning News.* He offered me $300 a month. I was shocked at the offer.

I did not have journalism experience but Walt stayed by my side and I learned from him. I covered everything from farming to social clubs and wedding and engagement announcements. And now, after 31 years at the biweekly *Reminder Morning News,* and the six-day-a-week *South Idaho Press,* I have learned much about news gathering and all that goes along with the profession of journalism.

Through the years, my husband, my daughter Sally and I have enjoyed traveling together. We have been across the United States and to several places abroad. I have kept active in the church, the community, and the Red Cross. I continue to share a close relationship with my mother, brothers and sisters and, of course, my children and six grandchildren.

I have no regrets for my life. I have always been content to be the age I am and I have never wished to live any of my life over. Each step along the way is a grand new adventure.

This is a wonderful land in which to live. And this is a wonderful and glorious time in history. Idaho is the choice state. I wouldn't want to live anywhere else. I am proud and fortunate to be an American.

Ruth Barnes Kunze

"Laugh, laugh, laugh,
and see the humor and irony in everything."

My German great-grandfather came to the United States to escape enforced military service. My great-grandmother came to work as a housemaid and refused to return home. Her brother came to take her home and he stayed too.

My English grandfather was a cabinet-maker and a respected craftsman. When his tools were stolen, he lost his trade. He went to work in a steel mill in Pittsburgh and eventually became the chief electrician.

The family history taught me that when one avenue is closed, we must choose or create a new one.

The Depression shaped my childhood. My father was denied a high school education (he went through the tenth grade). He worked in a wholesale bakery where he made everything by hand. He kneaded, cut and shaped doughnuts. He worked six days a week, at least twelve hours a day. We were very poor and I joke that we were made out of doughnuts. Our next-door neighbors had a produce market and they gave us damaged fruit and vegetables.

We learned to make do, redo, and mend and patch. Mother once took the shoestrings out of my shoes to make candlewicks.

We had an honor code that said we were obliged to share whatever we had. I remember tramps knocking on the back door and asking for food. No one was ever turned away. Usually Mom gave the men bread and gravy. I can still see each of them sopping up every drop with the crust. Today I have trouble discarding leftovers and my kids can tell you horror stories of how long I can make a turkey last.

I had two uncles in the service, which made my grandmother worry a lot. During World War II, my father's health kept him from military service but he switched to steel millwork for the war effort. He came home weary and dirty, no longer sweet smelling and with a dusting of flour.

Rationing kept our table sparse and we ate a lot of beans. We bought fresh food at a local farmer's market and walked home weighted down with seasonal produce.

We collected metals, paper and silver foil for the war effort. To purchase a tube of toothpaste, ointment or cream, an empty tube was exchanged for each purchase. (I remember that one woman without an exchange tube got her toothpaste squeezed into a sack). We never owned a car so gas rationing didn't directly affect us.

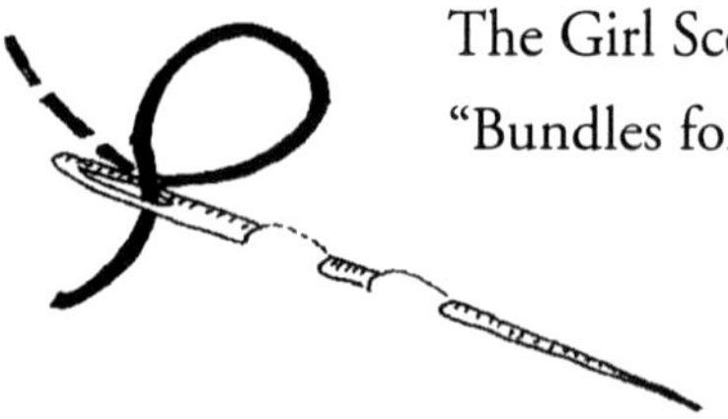

I learned to sew during the Great Depression. The Girl Scouts collected clothing and made "Bundles for Britain." These were care packages sent to Europe after the war. I helped to mend tattered clothing and sew patches on worn garments.

It took two years and seven different jobs to figure out how to work and pay my tuition for college. I stayed one month ahead of the tuition payments while I worked by giving science demonstrations and guided tours at the Buhl Planetarium in Pittsburgh. I scrounged for every scholarship I could find. These were not the days of financial aid and grants.

I commuted four hours a day and took up to twenty-one credits at one time. I changed universities and majors often so when I graduated in 1956, I had taken four years of college without an elective.

I had refused to take any secretarial or business courses while in school and I wasn't interested in the health professions, so only the teaching profession was open to me. Many school districts refused to interview me because I was engaged to be married but the Pittsburgh Public Schools did hire me because of my experience at the Planetarium.

I taught art and science in a departmentalized elementary school and I loved every day. It was a small, older school with only ten on the faculty including the librarian and the principal.

My second year there, the Board of Education interviewed the best science teachers for a position in the newly developing educational television. They wanted to format an elementary science television program for the Pittsburgh area.

My principal told me in front of the faculty at lunchtime that I was the best candidate for the job but I wasn't considered because I was a "biological hazard." (I was a recently married young woman who could become pregnant at anytime.) I was angry and insulted. The principal and friends tried to console me by saying that I should be grateful that I had been interviewed but I retorted that they should not have interviewed me when they had no intention of offering me the job. The year was 1957, which means that there was no recourse.

Being poor galled me and I railed against the lack of privilege. But I always knew that education was the ticket out. I never wanted charity. I wanted to earn my own way. I had learned not to rely on others' provisions.

My husband had a Ph.D. and I also wanted more than my Bachelor's degree. When he substituted for another professor on sabbatical, I instantly seized the opportunity to gain my Master's degree.

I could attend the University as a spouse for reduced fees. After carefully examining the course requirements, I realized that if I could drop the first course, I could finish in one year. So, again, I doubled up on credits and graduated from the University of Utah in August 1969 with a Master's of Educational Media.

With education came the understanding that it was important to move wherever the job could take me. In 1958, we moved from Pennsylvania to Idaho when my husband took a position with the National Reactor Testing Site, which is now the Idaho National Engineering and Environmental Lab (INEEL) in Idaho. We took a sightseeing trip along the old famous Route 66 all the way to California, then backtracked to Idaho. I wanted to see everything; historic places and beautiful scenery are my favorites.

I yearn to work with my hands. In Pittsburgh I taught elementary school art. Now I teach Community Education art classes, specializing in book arts. I have taken graduate art classes in pottery, sculpture, drawing, painting, book art and papermaking. The most rewarding times are when I am so involved that I become one with the work.

Along with the rewards of my life, there have also been challenges. The greatest challenge has been to stay true to my independent religious, political and social beliefs in the face of so much criticism. It is tough to be politically and religiously liberal. It has been difficult to stand for women's rights long before it became a popular issue, especially when my family, my workplace and my community did not support my ideas.

Every decision is a turning point. Every decision carries baggage that is part of the whole picture. The hardest thing to learn is how to let go of something or someone, and to trust that the growth and independence make us strong and capable.

Some important lessons I have learned through the years:

If one avenue closes, choose another or make one.

Nothing is ever really lost. You never know when or how you will use an experience but it is valuable, somewhere, sometime, somehow.

Everything is connected in spirit, in meaning, and in energy. Respect it.

My advice to all college students is to read the catalog and know what your requirements are and where you are going and find small scholarships and grants. They add up.

And most importantly laugh, laugh, laugh. See the humor and the irony in everything.

My knowledge and philosophy about life has affected not only my children but others as well. I am currently in the process of designing, illustrating and writing a book for my grandchildren that will incorporate my philosophy and lessons learned through my lifetime. I intend to stay connected with my children, grandchildren, and the community. I want to do something for others, which is bigger than I am.

A quote from Friederich Von Hugel strikes at the core of my being "...caring is the greatest thing, caring matters most." I want people to know that I care.

Thoughts are energy. And you can make your world or break your world by your thinking.

— Susan L. Taylor

Velma Morrison

"Be thankful you have your good health, your friends and your family."

I was born on August 1, 1920, in the San Joaquin Valley of California, the first of three children of Gladys Winsor and Earl Mitchell. My family were farmers near the township of Tipton and I grew up on the farm. My father's father bought the farm during the Gold Rush days. A lot of it is gone; we had to sell a little here and there over the years, but my son now lives there.

I am a child of the Depression. It was the during the dustbowl years and many people came to California, like in John Steinbeck's *The Grapes of Wrath.* My parents were landowners and we put many people up on different ranches and built tents for them to live in during the cold winters. It was a very poor time and no one had any money. That was when Hoover was president, and I remember the election of Roosevelt, and things turned to the better for many people.

I lived for a while in the area, going to school; I have fond memories of my classmates. Later, I went to a Las Vegas school and then into nurses training. I didn't finish because I got married and had my daughter Judith. That marriage didn't work out. Then World War II started and I became involved in the war effort. I was working in the shipyards of Richmond, California, along with a lot of other women, because the men were all off to war. I enjoyed the fact that we won and D-Day was all over. It was wonderful.

My life was truly changed by these events. After the war and all of this and that, my life got busy. I opened a large restaurant in Bakersfield, California, called The Broiler Steaks & Chops, and it could seat about a hundred and forty. I was doing very well there and business was good. That's where I met Mr. Morrison, and he came bringing the Governor and other people down to go to the football game because the Boise Junior College was in the same conference. This group of people came to eat at my restaurant. So my life was changed considerably. I was 37.

A few years went by and Harry Morrison and I were married on July 1, 1958. He told me that I shouldn't work so hard and after I married him, I never did work so hard again. We were very busy, traveling the world to see all the projects. Travel was fun in the beginning but exhausting later on. It was all business.

I had two sons from a previous marriage and they went to a military academy in Redwood City after we were married. My mother and her husband looked after them, living in our home in San Mateo. I would go there to visit with the children while Mr. Morrison took care of his work here in Idaho. My daughter was in college in San Francisco at the time. We were married for seventeen years until he passed away in 1971.

I have been very active in the community but I am now winding down. I sat for 23 years on the board at St. Luke's Hospital and worked with Albertson's College for 25 years, finally resigning from both positions a few years ago. I am phasing out of volunteer work because I believe I have done my fair share. I worked on the Board of Directors at Morrison Knudsen until I was seventy. Nevertheless, I continue to run our foundation and love doing the business things connected with it.

Any day is to be thankful that you have good health, your friends and your family. God has been good to me, considering that life is not always a bowl of cherries. I always remember a Robert Frost quote that I read, "Life is sort of an equalizer in its way, but for all the happiness that comes in a person's life, there is a toll to pay." For it all equals as we pass through.

I belong to the YMCA, the Rotary, and Fundsy. It is a program of auctioning things off that began when we were building the new YMCA downtown so we could put the windows in for the winter. It is a community thing and we still have it every two years. So far since the last Fundsy, they have given away over $20 million. They brought in approximately $375,000 at the last Fundsy. It's a good benefit.

I go to the First Methodist Church — the Cathedral of the Rockies. We have a great group of young people and we are starting a program to build another Sanctuary, just for what we call the "blue jeans group." Our church is growing and the young people, they just love it. And that's all well and good because our minister started that four or five years ago and it has just grown.

I recently celebrated my 80th birthday with a lavish party at the Morrison Center. There were around seven hundred people there and my dear friend, Fred Norman, put on a production. Then we showed the film of *My Fair Lady*, which we presented on stage when the Center opened fifteen years ago. My children were there and my son performed some songs that he had written for my birthday.

When I was younger, I wanted to accomplish everything that has happened in my life. Mr. Morrison taught me a lot; some of his integrity and all the good things he stood for rubbed off on me. No one is perfect; a person always has some regrets, but you can't look back. Just remember to be calm and gentle, love people, and make others happy. I think I have had a very good life. I am happy now, and God is in my life. I love my Lord with all my heart, with all my soul, with all my being. I don't think you can go it in this world alone. You must have the faith, the spirit, and the trust in God.

VERA NOYCE

"My office was between the tiger and zebra exhibits in a wide expanse of grass next to a small seasonal pond. It seems the perfect habitat for me."

I was born at 4:50 in the afternoon of July 5, 1939, in the Catholic hospital at Great Bend, Kansas. My mother was thirty-five years old and my father was fifty at the time of my birth. I have two older brothers who were eight and ten when I was born. My father had made a bargain with God regarding my birth; if a daughter were born, he would quit smoking cigarettes. I was and he did.

Until I was eight years old, we lived on a farm in Stafford County. My mother's immediate family lived there, all within a ten-mile radius. My grandfather lived in the middle of the family compound. My Uncle Park and his family lived across the road from Grandfather. My Aunt Sue's family of ten occupied a large house three miles to the north. And across the road from Sue lived my Aunt Jane, her husband and two sons. We lived half of a mile down the road from Jane. I had lots of cousins so there was always someone to play with.

We lived on a salt marsh, a wonderful wetland of brackish salt-water. Because the water was salty, we hauled drinking water from an artesian well a few miles from our house. There was a red-handled pump with a windmill and water for household use was collected in a cistern. We had no indoor plumbing and no electricity. We did have a telephone.

My brothers and cousins attended a one-room school, where the teacher taught grades one through eight. We raised most of our food. There was a large vegetable garden, fruit orchard, grapevines, honey-bees, chickens, turkeys, dairy cows, cattle, goats and sheep.

I remember the lake close to our house. I loved that lake. Cattails, reeds and grasses surrounded it and there was a small sandy beach at the north end. There was a cabin and duck blinds to accommodate hunters on the east shore and the rowboats used for net fishing were stored there.

I wasn't allowed to go to the lake alone but sometimes I just couldn't help myself. It was enchanting, mysterious and dangerous, promising adventure for a child. I would run down and look for frogs or listen to the birds. But Mother, who would be carrying a willow switch, would always find me.

Once, on the road, a blue racer snake chased me. Although these snakes are not poisonous, they are aggressive and can bite. You never knew when one of these creatures would show up on the path. There were many snakes, some of them poisonous. There were also a lot of porcupines, skunks, coyotes and badgers.

When Grandfather died in 1945, my parents moved to eastern Colorado. Grandfather had been the catalyst that kept the family together; soon after his death, the family scattered. My family moved to Stratton, Colorado. We kept our Kansas farm and leased it to a neighbor. The plains were very different from the salt marsh. It was dry, with few trees and flat land. I never liked it there. I missed my cousins and I missed the farm and lake.

In 1952, the U.S. Department of Interior purchased 22,000 acres of land in central Kansas to create the Quivira National Wildlife Refuge. The purchase included all of the property owned by my family, along with surrounding properties. Up until that time, we had visited frequently to keep an eye on the farm but after the sale, we stopped the visits. I didn't return until the fall of 1980.

Quivira is now very different from the place I remember as a young girl. All of the trees and buildings are gone. And the lake has disappeared. I am told that the refuge includes marshes, ranges, farmlands, and low sand hills. The area has returned to its natural state. There are at least 243 species of birds that have been sighted at the refuge. The habitat provides a place for waterfowl, shorebirds and marsh birds to nest. Sandhill cranes and bald eagles are abundant. And tourists such as the roadrunner and black-billed magpie have been seen there, which is out of their normal range.

Although I did not know it then, the wildness of the place with its abundance of wildlife would have a lasting effect on me. After working in a sterile, although beautiful high-rise building for ten years, I left a corporate job to work for the Idaho Zoological Society. My office was located between the tiger and zebra exhibits in a wide expanse of grass next to a small seasonal pond. It seems to be the perfect habitat for me.

While the young girl inside of me sometimes misses her childhood home, the adult environmentalist is delighted. As more of the country is developed, and more wildlife habitat is destroyed, refuges like Quivira can mean the difference between life and death, sometimes for an entire species.

While I sit and gaze through my kitchen window in Idaho, I can still see a mockingbird resting on a cattail near a lake and singing with joy in the Kansas sunset. And I am a child once again.

Alice Laan

"When I was approached to submit a biography for ELDER TALES, my initial reaction was: Elder? When did that happen?"

I was born in Berkhout, Holland, on May 14, 1932, to Pieter and Elisabeth Visser. I was the eldest of five children and the only girl. I attended school in Berkhout. Later I attended school in Hoorn, Holland, specializing in Home Economics. Upon graduating, I continued my education by obtaining my degree in Tailoring and Fine Needle Arts.

During my youth, World War II was going strong. Life in Europe was difficult. We always heard word of when the German soldiers would be coming through our town. They would come right into the classroom to ensure that our teachers were not lecturing on the evils of Nazism.

My family showed defiance toward the Nazis by hiding a member of the Dutch Underground. Jaap helped my father on the family farm to earn his keep and also to maintain a low profile. We heard the word when the Germans would be conducting house searches to enlist young men to help further their cause. My father and brothers would hide

Jaap in a crawl space under the kitchen floor. We had a rug that we put over the trapdoor. My mother would place me in a chair over the hidden door and place a bowl of potatoes upon my lap. She would instruct me to peel and stay quiet while she spoke to the German soldiers. There I would be rocking and peeling, and praying that Jaap would not be found beneath the brittle chair I sat upon.

My best friend, Aaf, introduced me to her second cousin in 1950. His name was Rein Laan. He was tall, dark and handsome. I fell for him immediately. We dated for a while. I soon discovered that Rein's dream was to move to America. His brother Klaas lived in the United States with his wife and two children. Klaas wanted his brother to join him. He found a sponsor for us who would be willing to employ my husband on his farm. Rein asked if I would become his wife and move with him to America. We were married on October 8, 1953, in Berkhout, Holland. It was a difficult time for me. I was not only a new bride but I would be leaving my homeland and my family behind. I felt the thrill of excitement, but also felt the fear of the unknown.

We were on the boat for ten days. We left Holland on February 19, 1954, and arrived in New York City on the first of March. The Atlantic Ocean was not calm and I was seasick the entire trip. Upon arrival, I told my husband that I would never step foot on a boat again. Forty-five years later I remain true to my word.

We made our way to Grand Central Station and departed on the train to Chicago. It was in the windy city that I experienced my first hamburger. We then embarked on the Portland Rose and made our way across the United States. I remember gazing out of the window, looking at nothing but snow. There was not a building or house in sight. We were in the middle of Wyoming. I remember thinking, what have I got myself into?

We reached our destination, Nyssa, Oregon, at midnight on March 4, 1954. Klaas and his family were there to pick us up. At last there was someone who could speak our language.

We settled in Adrian, Oregon. We learned the English language by listening to the radio and reading our niece's schoolbooks. One of the first words I learned, I picked up from my husband who had picked it up from a co-worker. I remember that I used this word while speaking with a kind neighbor. After I gracefully intertwined it into my sentence, the woman asked if I knew what it meant. I shook my head. She took me by the hand to the corral, pointed at some manure and said, "That is what your word means and nice ladies do not use it." That was my first and most humiliating English grammar lesson.

Our daughter Catherina Elisabeth was born on May 11, 1955. My days were spent taking care of her, keeping the house clean, cooking and sewing. Then on July 25, 1958, we had our second daughter, Marianne Reina. But our family was not complete until March 22, 1962, when our twin sons were born, Pieter Klaas and Ray Johannes Laan. We were surprised. We were expecting one, not two.

In 1965, we moved to Parma, Idaho, and remained there until 1974 when we moved to our present home in Caldwell.

In 1974, I decided that it was time to explore the job market. I had an interest in Real Estate. But I discovered that in order to become licensed as an agent, I would have to get my General Education Degree. It took two tries before I passed the exam but that wasn't the end of it. It took five tries before I finally passed the Real Estate examination. This

was an exercise not only in futility, but humility as well. I have learned that perseverance and stubbornness are two of my strongest traits. I worked with Karn Real Estate for seventeen years. I retired from Jensen Real Estate in 1996.

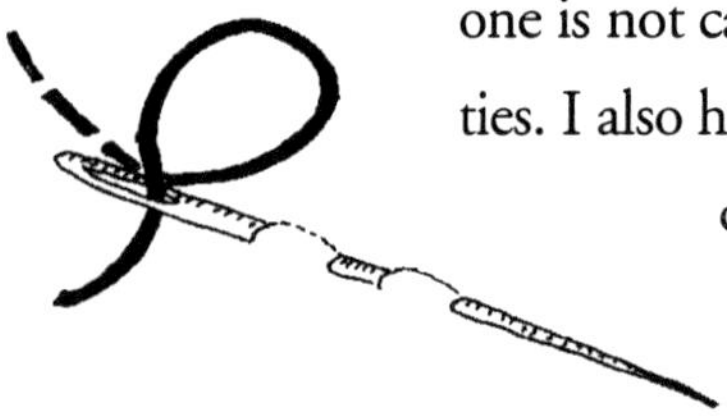

Retirement is wonderful but can lead to boredom if one is not careful. I belong to many clubs and sororities. I also have several hobbies to occupy my time. I quilt, do needlepoint, sew, paint, garden, and usually spend a lot of time with my eight (soon to be nine) grandchildren.

My life has been ordinary but tempered with just enough melodrama to keep it interesting. I never know what is around the corner and can only hope I continue to experience all the good things life has to offer. Who knows, perhaps someday I'll live out my dream and attend art school in Amsterdam.

Betty Luginbill

"Things won't always be better in the morning; they may be worse. But they will be different and the process is fascinating."

I was married to my husband for twenty-five years before I became a widow due to an accident that took his life. My husband was an officer in the Navy during World War II when we met. After we had been together for a few years, the children began to arrive. We had three boys and one girl, who are now married and parents to my nine grandchildren. I am pleased that each of my children chose to follow the word of God and to raise their children to do the same.

I spent my children's growing years at home. But as each left for college, I decided to do the same. I had gone to school before I was married. I attended the University of Wisconsin and received a Bachelor of Science degree in Home Economics and went on to Purdue to receive a Master's of Science in Food and Nutrition. But in the early 1970s as the children were leaving, I decided to attend Wesley Theological Seminary and Scarritt University in Nashville. I received a Master's degree in Christian Education. My last

educational stop was Garrett Evangelical Theological Seminary in Evanston where I received a Master's of Divinity Degree.

My studies gave me the opportunity to become a Campus Minister in Eugene, Oregon. I was there for one year then moved to Fairbanks, Alaska, and worked as an Associate Pastor in the First United Methodist Church. In 1981, I moved to southern Oregon and was a pastor for two churches. I was asked to move to Boise to pastor a small church. I graciously accepted the offer because my youngest son and his family lived here. I retired from the church in Boise after five years. I have been volunteering since.

I am in the healing field with The International Order of St. Luke, the physician, with the idea of restoring the healing of Jesus (the laying on of hands, healing of memories or inner healing) within the church. I also work with Walk to Emmaus in the capacity of pastor, and Church Women United as a state officer in the Legislative Action area, and as acting president of the Ada County CWU. I continue to preach and counsel.

I chose the career in Home Economics because I had been in 4-H and didn't have much vision beyond the farm. And besides, that's what girls were supposed to know; and if they didn't, they had better learn. The second career of becoming a Director of Christian Education and a pastor and healer was because I was called to do so.

I did not encounter obstacles in my career until I became a pastor. I learned then what discrimination and harassment meant. I had worked in Race Relations for five years in the Maryland area outside of Washington, D.C. I had seen and heard about how difficult it was for a woman but until I experienced being a woman in a male-dominated profession, I did not fully understand the meaning of the words. Gender bias did affect me. I had to learn how to cope with this discrimination or I would have never made it past my first year in the profession.

My husband was a Research Administrator for the Department of Agriculture. It was his job to review research projects from all over the United States. So he would include the children and me on various trips. As a result, I have been in all of the fifty states. My travel as a minister has taken me to Australia, Africa, Europe, Asia, Mexico, and Israel. I remember one trip to Europe. I brought my daughter and we traveled the countries on $15 a day. It can be done.

I enjoy singing and dancing. I sing with a group and do some line dancing every once in a while. But mostly these days I enjoy reading and writing. I stay quite active in the church and have maintained my title as a Political Activist. I am involved in several organizations, which take a lot of my time. These include the United Methodist Church, the Sweet Home Rotary Club, the Boise Southwest Rotary Club, Church Women United, United Vision of Idaho, International Order of St. Luke, Capital Contribution Center and BIG, Beltsville Interracial Group.

I stay quite active for my seventy-three years. I was taught to work hard and stay involved with life. I was born with a natural perseverance that ran in the family. I have been blessed.

I have learned that loving, caring, forgiving, and working toward the helping and healing of people and the planet, is essential to maintaining a good life. I have also learned that God can be trusted even if all else fails. And that people have far more talent and ability than they often realize. Sometimes things won't always be better in the morning, they may be worse, but they will be different and the process is fascinating.

In the future, I expect to learn more about healing through the power of Jesus and the Holy Spirit. I am content with my life but I must not be too content. Because I have found that every time I get completely satisfied with the way that things are going in my life, some big change occurs and I must learn new ways of coping and expanding my horizons. But that is what makes the world an exciting place to live.

I love God and I love His people.

Mary Milton

*"Although we had lots of hard times,
we always had laughter and songs in our heart."*

My Irish grandparents came to the United States and farmed in Iowa. My mother graduated from high school a few years after arriving in the country. At twenty, my mother married my father. Together they had eight children. I was born on September 16, 1903. I have four brothers and three sisters.

When I was very young, my father moved the family to South Dakota. All he saw in the state was what he called "gumbo land." So he moved us to Nebraska and bought a farm. I was Dad's right hand because each of my brothers was earning money for college. All four desired to practice medicine. Dad and I farmed for several years, then I too received my education in teaching.

I became a teacher in a small Nebraska town. I taught for a few years before I met Howard Milton, who was a local rancher. We married in 1926 and I stayed home to raise our three sons and four daughters.

In 1930, we moved to Wyoming. We had three children at the time. Upon arriving we decided to build a house. I remember one day that Howard took his old truck to town to buy some lumber to begin the house. When he returned he unloaded his wood on a path, not knowing that it was an antelope trail. The next morning he went to start our house and found that the antelope had pawed and chopped the lumber into pieces. It was scattered everywhere. But just months later he had built us a small four-room house.

At the house, we built a cistern (a tank for storing water). We hauled water in a barrel from a neighbor's well on a sled pulled by a horse and usually spilled half on the way home. When it rained, we would catch what we could. And when it snowed, we would scrape it off the sides of the house and use it for washing and cleaning the house. So it wasn't as easy as turning on a faucet. Fuel also was hard to get. We would take a hay rake and gather cow chips. The chips make a very hot fire, which we used to heat the water.

Our nearest neighbors were a few miles away. Sometimes they would hold dances in their barn. I remember one night when the family was ready to go but the old pick-up wasn't. So Howard attached two boxes to a team of horses and we sat in the boxes while the horses pulled us the few miles up the road.

During the Depression, times were hard. Cattlemen drove their cattle to market. The trail they used was across our land. Six cowboys were driving their herd to market one evening when a Negro got off and came to the house and asked for a slice of bread. I had to refuse him because I didn't have enough for my own family. That was hard.

During those tough years, Howard worked for anyone who needed help. After a few months of odd jobs, Howard was hired to farm potatoes and run cattle. The children were all in school at the time and a bus took them the fifty miles each way. They left in the dark and returned in the dark. The girls wore flour sack dresses, which I made.

Times slowly got better. I enjoyed living on the farm, and gardening and canning. We had enough food to feed our seven children. And sometimes even extra to feed a Sunday guest now and then.

As the war began, our sons enlisted in the military service. Dale joined the Navy and Ralph went into the Marines. Ralph was a jeep driver for Colonel Beall during the Korean War. Our youngest son Roland also joined the Marines. We were lucky; each one came back the way he went in.

From Wyoming we moved to Twin Falls, Idaho, where Howard continued farming. Years later we moved to Nampa, Idaho, and Howard opened a small business as a Custom Farmer. He would travel to farms and fields with his own machinery and harvest for the owner. Within a couple of years, Howard lost his leg in an accident and that same year, he became ill. At the onset of Howard's illness I had been employed for fifteen years at the Idaho State School for Retarded Children. I retired to take care of him. We moved to Boise to be closer to doctors and the hospital. In 1983, I lost my husband and our eldest daughter Jessie.

Although we have had lots of hard times, we always had laughter and songs in our heart. The children have a family reunion each year on my birthday. They have been doing this since 1953. And with seven children, seventeen grandchildren, thirty-three great-grandchildren, and two great-great-grandchildren, it's a big reunion.

We have to improve life, not just for those who have the most skills and those who know how to manipulate the system. But also for and with those who often have so much to give but never get the opportunity

— Dorothy Height

Esther Simplot

"We must work hard, discipline ourselves,
and be responsible for our actions.
Life is not easy. Work is not easy.
But hard work and commitment do and will pay off."

I was born on November 17, 1934, to lovely parents who were farmers in Wisconsin. I was the sixth of seven children, so we had an animated childhood with the ups and downs of sibling rivalries. We also had our chores: weeding the garden and hoeing potatoes (which is a joke on me now that I am married to the Potato King). It was a poor family, but we were happy and always had enough to eat.

When I started elementary school, I walked two miles each way to a one-room schoolhouse; in the winter, the snow was piled high on the banks. These years passed quickly. I loved horses, so I drove the work-horses for my father until we finally got a tractor. One year, my parents bought me a cow pony. It was my job to ride out into the pasture and gather up all the cows to be milked.

I admire the young women of today, trying to balance careers, husbands and family. I don't know where they get the energy but I appreciate the hard work they go through in order to keep balance. My mother kept the farm in balance. Even though she did not do as much physical work as my father, she was responsible for keeping the books, accounting for all the money earned and spent. She also took care of the house, a husband and a family. My parents worked as a team.

About the time World War II began, the farm was beginning to recover from the Depression and the money was beginning to come in. I'll never forget one Christmas when my mother blindfolded me, stood me on the kitchen table and pinned up two dresses to hem. She wrapped each one and put them under the tree. These were my Christmas gifts, the most I had ever received up until then.

I went to a small high school with about two hundred students, but we had wonderful and dedicated teachers. The teachers loved the students and they inspired us to do well and always set a fine example of moral values. We wanted to do good; not only to please ourselves, but also the teachers whom we admired. I was always the first to participate in school programs. My sister and I were quite active in class plays, the band and chorus. I played the clarinet and she played the trumpet.

I loved to sing, and my vocal talent was recognized the last year of high school. The band director encouraged me to try out for musical parts in school plays and then, as the school year drew to a close, he pushed for me to attend college and major in music. I was valedictorian and out of the fifty-two in my graduating class, I was the only one who went to college.

The college was an all women's school in Illinois. I majored in music, voice and public school education. After college, I used my teaching skills to obtain a job in the Chicago school district. Within two years, I paid off my student loans, which makes me quite proud even today. I shared an apartment with another woman in Evanston, Illinois, which made it a little easier to save money.

Teaching was not easy for me. I taught in a very affluent area of

Chicago where the children were used to having everything they wanted. I remember a teacher who taught fifth grade had a nervous breakdown soon after I arrived. Her classroom was just across the hall from mine. I had over eight hundred music students that first year and they were a handful for a 21-year-old teacher. A lot of students were in their teens, so some of them were almost as old as I was. I had to memorize their names and grade all the tests. It was not an easy task but a responsibility and a challenge nonetheless. I am still not sure how I survived that first year, but I did, and continued for another year.

After the second year of teaching, I began to lose my voice and I was afraid that singing would be out if I didn't stop teaching. Singing was my first love and teaching came next. I remember talking to my singing coach. I'll never forget her response: "Esther, go to New York. Just quit teaching and go to New York to pursue your desire to sing." I had no money in the bank and I realized I shouldn't even entertain the thought. But I took her advice and left for New York. All I had as I boarded the train were my belongings, the name of a voice coach, and the name of a landlord who might have a room.

When I arrived at Grand Central Station, I put my suitcase in a locker and got on a bus, to go to the top of the Empire State Building and survey the city that was to be my home for ten years. Then I returned for my suitcase and followed the directions to the landlord's house. The woman had a room so I was able to stay in my new place on my first night in New York. Within two days, I had a job and began voice lessons.

During those ten years, I worked on becoming an opera singer or what was called Concert Stage, which was a singer who had a piano accompaniment. The wonderful classic songs are seldom done today, which saddens me greatly. I also studied ballet and language. But I decided my talent was not what was required to become a professional singer. By that time, I had met my husband, packed my belongings and moved to Denver.

I had worked with a woman in New York who called me Cinderella after I had married my husband. She knew me when I was poor and had to work so diligently and she watched me as I began to travel the world and experience a life I had only dreamed of before. I did feel a little like Cinderella.

I think one of the reasons Mr. Simplot and I got along so well is that we were both farmers. We both grew up on a farm and we both know the meaning of hard work. When you come from that sort of background, there are no pretenses. You know that life is not always easy and when good things happen, they are appreciated and not taken for granted.

One of my proudest moments came in 1972, when I was asked to sing the National Anthem at a Washington Huskies football game. The Huskies won and went on to play in the Rose Bowl, inviting me along to sing again. It was exciting to stand on the field and look out at the spectators. Believe it or not, I wasn't a bit nervous. The game was broadcast on television and I remember my poor mother — who had never watched a football game in her life — telling me how she sat there and watched for me. Unfortunately, I was never shown to television viewers.

Besides my interest in singing, I have a grand passion for riding horses. I ride English and I've learned to jump quite well. I began riding when everyone my age was quitting. I continue to ride to this day — I competed in dressage this summer, and did very well. I ride simply for pleasure.

Community has always been important to me. When I came to Boise, one of my first thoughts was, "What can I do for the community to enhance the arts, music and culture of this beautiful city?" For the first few years, I joined the Boise Opera and kept quite active but I always wanted to do more. It was about this time that the Morrison Center was built and I thought about the possibility of buying a building for rehearsals. Up until this time, the performers never had a place to call their own; rehearsals took place at donated sites, which was difficult for the crew. I felt that our lovely city needed a rehearsal theater. The search for a building continued for a long time until my daughter-in-law discovered the perfect place. I fell in love with it, my husband purchased it and the renovation began. The Boise Opera, Boise Philharmonic, and Ballet Idaho all make their home there now.

I've always had a goal. Whether it was going to college, pursuing my singing, or growing in a job, there has always been motivation within me to succeed. Sometimes things don't happen the way you want them to or think they will, but they have a way of working out. We walk through the door and if the other side is not what we had anticipated, we proceed because other doors will begin to open.

One of my greatest inspirations has been my husband. I have learned a great deal from Mr. Simplot, one of the most important being finance. All I knew before I met J.R. was that bills must be paid and that you didn't spend more than you had. It seemed easy. I didn't know much about saving money because I didn't have the extra to do so. He has taught me about saving and investing and thinking ahead. It is obvious today that parents and schools are not teaching the children about the necessity of saving because Americans are not saving.

So how does one save and prepare for the future? How do we use what we make to the best advantage? It's all about discipline, priorities and choices. Money is a big responsibility. It is important that we learn how to distribute the money so that it is used in a positive way. I have often said, "It's so much easier being a secretary."

It is important that children work and receive compensation for their time. This teaches us about productivity and instills a high self-esteem. If someone works for something, then they will be proud not only of the monetary compensation, but the accomplishment of a job well done. If children never have to work and receive everything without giving of themselves, then how can there be a feeling of self-worth? I believe this is why so many of our rich people are so unhappy — they do not feel they have a life of any significance.

We must work hard, discipline ourselves, and be responsible for our actions. Life is not easy. Work is not easy. But hard work and commitment do and will pay off. I think that my husband and I are proof of that.

Margaret Martinez

"Life is good even with all of the trials and tribulations we face day by day. But with hope and joy in our hearts, we can overcome the obstacles."

It was a hot day in 1926 and the town seemed still and lazy. The screaming sirens interrupted the stillness of the day, as the ambulance stopped in front of the house. Suddenly, the street became alive with noise and curious onlookers watched as the ambulance attendant brought out a lifeless woman.

The patient was rushed to the hospital and into the emergency ward. Soon the doctors came out and talked to the woman's distraught husband. "Mr. Weber," the doctor said, "we are doing everything to save your wife and child but I do not have a lot of hope." And that is the way it was on July 21, 1926, moments after I entered the world. I was considered a miracle. I weighed two pounds. And Mother and I both recovered from the traumatic ordeal.

No one was more thrilled than Mom and Dad to see me take my first step one week before my first birthday. My steps proved to my parents that I was not a paralytic. I could now begin to keep up with my siblings, Fritz, age four: Lilo, age five; and Sofie, age eight.

During a visit to our home, Dr. Wolf noticed that my eyes did not focus correctly. He scheduled an appointment to run some tests. It was late in August 1927 in Dr. Wolf's office when Mom and Dad learned that I was blind.

I had the loving support from my family. My parents assured me that I could achieve any goal that I set for myself. I was unaware that I was different from anyone else until the age of ten when my schoolmates began to taunt me, which left me very confused.

With maturity, I became more aware of the new changes brought to our lives by the politics of Adolph Hitler. Times were prosperous but all too soon there was austerity because of the preparations for war. Our lives were beginning to change and were now filled with terror and uncertainty.

Our home in Frankfurt was destroyed by the war and I was evacuated to a farming village all alone. This was devastating because I now fully realized the extent of my blindness. I was faced with surviving by my own abilities. I walked eight miles to and from the train station in all types of weather. I used a stick to guide me.

One day during an air raid, people rushed in hordes to the railroad station bunker and I had the misfortune to be on the stairs. I was trampled by hundreds of people. I hung on to a man's trouser leg and he pulled me from the chaos and probably saved my life.

When the war ended, I was reunited with my family in Frankfurt. We began the task of rebuilding our lives and the city, which was almost destroyed.

It was difficult for me to appreciate the soldiers who occupied our city for there was much bitterness in my heart. We had lost nine family members during the war. Many of my friends were fraternizing with the American GIs, but I would not. My mother reassured me that it was neither their fault nor our fault that a war broke out, and that each side had a duty.

Soon after my mother's tearful words, I met an American soldier one Sunday afternoon at the city zoo. His name was Paul Martinez.

Over the next several months Paul and I became good friends. But then it was time for him to return to the United States. He assured me that he would be back.

In September 1946, the doorbell rang and there was Paul. He gave me a ring and asked my father for my hand in marriage. We were married in February 1947. We were one of the firsts German/American couples to be granted permission to marry.

We celebrated our last Christmas with my family in Germany and the greatest gift was our son, Freddy. He was born on December 20, 1947. After the holidays, preparations began for our departure from Germany in April 1948.

The sea voyage was not a pleasure cruise. We were on a military transport vessel. Many war brides with babies were on board. The men and their wives were segregated due to military regulations. I shared a cabin with two women and Freddy.

The Statue of Liberty finally came into view. I was told all about its history as its looks were described to me. It thrilled me and gave me hope for a new life. I just wished that I could see it.

Upon our arrival, Paul had to report to Fort Sill, Oklahoma. He left me behind with his family in Salt Lake City, Utah, while he found housing for us. Preparations were made for Freddy and me to join him in Lawton, Oklahoma. I had not anticipated that my mother-in-law would decide to live with us in Oklahoma. It was a difficult journey east for all three of us. My mother-in-law spoke no English and my

Spanish, mingled with Italian, was of little use. Here I was alone in a strange country, with shadow vision and limited funds, traveling for miles and miles on a train with a mother-in-law I hardly knew and could not communicate with.

My first home in America was little more than a shack. Although we made the best of a difficult situation, I was happy to learn that in just a few months we would be returning to Salt Lake.

We moved next door to Paul's family. Our goal was that after Paul completed his education, we would buy our own home, no matter how small and humble. Paul worked diligently at a part-time job while attending school. I was lucky to have one hour a day with him.

We finally moved into our house and soon after our move we were blessed with a second child, a beautiful little red-haired girl. We named her Theresa.

In 1955, my life took a new turn when I found an ophthalmologist who fitted me with contact lenses specially designed for my needs. Once I got the contact lenses in my eyes, which was no easy task, the world was an awesome place for me. It was the first time in my life I was able to vaguely see the faces of my children and husband. The concept of color was introduced to me and things took on new meaning.

That same year, my husband took us back to Germany to visit my parents. My new appearance changed had me so that they did not recognize me when they met us at the airport. As soon as they saw Paul, they came hurrying toward us. It was the first time for me to see their loving faces.

The following years of our lives brought many difficulties but also great joy. Paul interrupted his studies and began a full-time job, which led us to a transfer to Idaho in 1959. The name of the town, Mountain

Home, sounded beautiful. But to this day, I still look for the mountains in Mountain Home.

In 1960, I realized there was no kindergarten in the small rural town. I had always loved spending time with my children and their friends, playing games, reading books and singing songs. So I decided it was time for me to fulfill my lifelong dream of teaching. At Boise State University I challenged subjects that I had taken in my former education. I was granted credit for them and received a list of courses that would qualify me for certification in Idaho as a teacher. I received my degree after two years. In 1961, I opened a private kindergarten.

Happy Day Kindergarten occupied our daylight basement and was filled so quickly that even at the beginning, we had long waiting lists. Soon we had to make more space, which cost Paul his garage. Our kindergarten held morning and afternoon sessions with four teachers and a school bus.

My sight began to diminish in 1972 and by 1974, I was forced to go into a rehabilitation program through the Idaho Commission for the Blind. This period was difficult for now I knew the pleasure of sight, but I thank God for the memories of that time when I did see.

In 1987, I retired and closed the doors of Happy Day Kindergarten. After retirement, I continued to cast about for something meaningful to do. I facilitated a group of visually impaired seniors, helping them to find alternative ways to cope with their visual disability. We attended a workshop at the Commission for three weeks in which I chose to take an accelerated writing course. It was during this time that I decided to create a cookbook for the visually impaired. I shared my favorite recipes, requiring only six ingredients or less, and designed a cookbook, complete with vinyl pages, which would safeguard the book from spills. The book was published in August 1996.

After the accomplishment of the cookbook, I decided it was time to take out the manuscript I had written about my life which had lain hidden for many years. I decided that I could finish it with the use of a talking computer. I was often asked why I would start this now at seventy. My answer was that Grandma Moses started to paint at seventy. If she can do it, so can I. The book was published in July 1999.

Life is good even with all of the trials and tribulations we face day by day. But with hope and joy in our hearts, we can overcome the obstacles. I have many more things planned for the coming years that I hope will be beneficial to others.

I will leap into the new millennium with thankfulness to God for guiding me through each day. I look forward as I use my life to the best of my ability.

Dorris Murdock

"Peace is not needing to know what is going to happen next."

I used to get upset with people who said, "All you need is faith." I discovered that wasn't enough when my marriage of thirty-five years was destroyed along with my dream of being wife and mother. I had done it all, nurturing my husband and four children, putting their needs before mine all of my life, only to discover it wasn't enough.

My husband walked out of the divorce settlement after four years and I had no recourse. I was given a two-month notice that I would suddenly have no income. My husband had never allowed me to be employed outside the home and now he said I should go to work and support myself. My only job while being married was to make my husband happy and I realized that was an impossible task, for we cannot make others internally happy, that must come from within.

Faced with financial disaster, I searched the farthest reaches of my faith and decided that obviously I was not in charge of life but felt that someone else was. I decided to let go and allow the spirit to move in whatever way She would, feeling that She knew more about what I needed than I. I was released from fear and freed to move ahead with confidence.

Peace is not the need to know what is going to happen next.

For a while I took any job that came along but soon found a job as a medical transcriber. I continue to work in my own transcribing business. I do not have a retirement plan but I am not afraid of the future; in fact, I am ready for each day. I sleep well, knowing that She is awake.

It is all right for me to be me. It is all right for you to be you.

I once read a book entitled, *Please Understand Me.* It changed the way I looked at others and myself. From it, I discovered that there are four types of people in the world. I came to understand and accept myself and those around me.

As a result, I wanted to have another opportunity to have a loving relationship. I attended my 50th college reunion in May 1998. I met a man who was in my class in 1944. His wife had died the previous year. We corresponded by Email for several months and then decided to meet and see whether we wanted to proceed with our relationship. The result was our wedding in March 1999. We are now enjoying each day together.

We attract to ourselves the experience we need in order to become the person we can become.

We may choose to refuse to enter into any given experience, but if we do, it will show up in a different way. So I welcome events, even an unpleasant experience, because I know it is there for my growth.

Forgiveness is possible and necessary.

I struggled with anger at my husband and at the church who treated me negatively during the divorce ("it was her fault … she was too pushy"). When I thought it through, I realized that if my husband could have been different, he would have been. We do what we do for who we are at that moment in our lives; if we could do differently, we would. And so in believing this, I forgave him. But more importantly I forgave myself for any pain that I may have caused.

We all want unconditional love.

Accepting that people do what they do because that is who they are at that moment in their life allows me to accept other people as they are without requiring that they be different. It is the way to unconditional love in a marriage, not demanding that we change, only that we accept each other as we are.

If you want something enough, you will make it happen.

I desire to leave something of myself behind when I leave this earth. I wrote my first book when I had four children under four years old. I would put them down for naps and work on my book. Later I wrote my story of living ten years in West Africa on the mission field, *Storm of the Soul,* which was published in 1999. My next book is *Journey of the Soul.*

And so my seventy-two years have brought me to the place where I know I am loved, first and most importantly by myself, but now by a soul mate, my husband. My life has only just begun, again, as it has several times when I have had to pull it together and go on. I hope that in my

writing, as well as in other opportunities, I can help women discover that it is all right to be whoever we are, not just all right, but unique and special.

Clara Posey

"I have enjoyed a good life, and the hardships of my youth have made me strong and resilient."

I was born in 1923 at Robinson, North Dakota. My childhood was happy and it holds many fond memories.

I received my high-school education in a class of eight students. I married Lyle in 1941 at the age of eighteen and we had three lovely children. I have enjoyed a good life and the hardships of my youth have made me strong and resilient.

None of the amenities we enjoy or take for granted today existed when I was a young woman. Lignite coal heated my prairie home and cooking stove. Heavy, home-sewn quilts often had frost on them when I awoke on cold winter mornings. Without plumbing, water for household use and bathing was carried from a well, thirty yards from the house. To preserve meat, I wrapped and stored beef and pork in a barrel next to the house. If any meat was left by

springtime I canned it, because we didn't have refrigeration. Winters were extreme with snow measured by the foot. Trips to town were made with a horse-drawn sleigh and required bundling during harsh winter rides. Other seasons, tractors were used for transportation. Everyone looked forward to signs of spring.

Farming was laborious and women worked beside men. I shocked grain from fields, hauled hay, milked cows and fed calves and chickens. Milk was run through a separator. In the fall, eight or nine threshers were hired and I cooked for all the men. Veterinarians were not readily available, requiring me to assist with birthing of calves. We didn't have television so when the chores were done for the day, the entertainment was usually to gather around the radio, play card games, dance, watch ballgames or movies, make homemade ice cream and visit family and friends. Relatives encouraged us to move west to avoid the harsh North Dakota winters, so Lyle and I moved when the children were in their teens. I worked as a bank teller and Lyle worked as a golf course greens keeper.

When the fifties era arrived, new adventures and conveniences came too, but my greatest and fondest memories were of my early years with loved ones in North Dakota.

Dr. Mamie Oliver

"As I contemplate the balance of life's journey I find that I must look inward using faith and backward to draw on the influences found in family, ancestors, and cultural community."

I was born in Natchez, Mississippi, a radically segregated state. My family lived near the small town of Natchez on a rural small farm in Cannonsburg, Mississippi. Black children in the thirties and forties in Mississippi lived in an all black lifestyle. The schools I attended were all black. And if we went downtown, we could only drink from a water fountain marked, "Colored only." We seldom went to town except on weekends. All the store clerks were white. The movie houses would only permit black children to sit in a designated area upstairs in the theater.

My nurturing was done by an extended family of relatives and by the women at the church. In the country, now described as the rural, my childhood was laced with chapters of adventure. Thankfully, the surroundings could be described as an environmentally natural setting. It was near the famous Natchez Trace; wooded, green and crowded with animals, gardens, fruit trees, snakes, birds, hot sun, rain, thunder, lightning and clouds. In such a setting I felt the comfort and soothing calm akin to hope and happiness. Blessed are all birds and animals, the wildest beasts and yes, all serpents too for they live in nature in a state of natural grace. They live beyond the rules of evil and good. Their instincts are obedient to these laws and they suffer no shame, regret, or sin. Nor do they curse failures of themselves. How much I have learned from my early years of being in that environment, for the wild creatures harbor no evil toward one another, and they trust their own inner sense of how to live. Yes, they are blessed. I have come to know that I am also. Life's journey has had some pain and some laughter, but out of both came a song, lots of growth and even a few gray hairs.

The offspring of a single mother, I was the youngest of two female children. Mother valued education and literally took me from the state of Mississippi to California after she married. In California, she enrolled me in elementary school, gave me the opportunity to take piano lessons and raised me as an only child. My maternal grandmother raised my sister. Values were a must in my family. Emphasis was placed on self-sufficiency and responsibility. My mother tried to be a role model. With a minimal education, she worked hard, often in service areas like bakeries, retail stores, school cafeterias, and clothing manufacturing industries. The values I learned helped propel me in life. As the first woman in my family to pursue higher education, I was evidence that a new era had begun.

The experience of summer camp, church group work, music and athletic challenge all contribute to my personal growth. I played tennis in high school and college. Being with other women and establishing friendships and networks was strengthening.

I have learned that where there is pain, to use it. All things pass. We must find our spirit side. Let it be the influence for life's challenges. There is a flesh side but unless you crucify this side, you can frequently get sidetracked. Mistakes can be like wounds, but refuse to linger there. Live in the real world but let the fruit of the spirit grow you into maturity.

The journey of life requires that we pay our dues. How does one do that? Marian Wright Edelman once said that, "You pay your dues with effort, earn rewards with work, make oneself necessary, indeed indispensable." In the life of Black Americans historically, if we wanted to get ahead, we had to do more than was needed before it was asked, do it well without expecting huge praise, and understand that freedom was not free.

We are encouraged to get up when we fall. We must act in faith when uncertainties come. In these times of setbacks, it is in God's faithfulness that we trust. There is no time for self-pity. Individual struggle for some women and Black Americans specifically is part of an ongoing struggle for freedom and justice that must be won over and over again.

Prayer is powerful and the seeds of faith will reply. Persevere, work, and serve. We must remember to lift others as we individually climb.

Mamie Oates Oliver, BA, M.S.W., Ph.D., has been involved in human services work for over forty years. Dr. Oliver is a graduate of Los Angeles State College, Los Angeles, California; Fresno State University, Fresno, California; and Washington State University, Pullman, Washington. She has conducted workshops and seminars on human issues and concerns. As a people person, she is often called upon to speak for women's groups, churches and civic organizations. She also serves as a consultant to businesses, health systems, and families.

Dr. Oliver is interested in social issues that affect children, families, women, ethnically diverse persons, and the aged.

The Idaho Statesman has recognized Dr. Oliver as a distinguished citizen. She was honored by the Boise March of Dimes as one of ten Outstanding Women in Idaho. She was appointed by Governor John

Evans to be the Chair of Idaho's Special Task Force Committee commemorating the first national holiday honoring the life and works of Dr. Martin Luther King, Jr. Dr. Oliver has also received the Social Worker of the Year Award by the Central Branch of National Association of Social Workers of Boise.

During her professional career, Dr. Oliver worked as a social worker for Los Angeles County, Los Angeles, California, in the department of adoptions, Aid to Families with Dependent Children and for the Mental Health Department. In Washington, she worked as a hospital social work director at Holy Family Hospital and then she helped to develop the mental health program for the Spokane County Commissioners. In 1972, Mamie moved to Boise, Idaho. In Boise she was an Assistant and Associate Professor in the Department of Social Work at Boise State University. She served on the Board of Directors of the YMCA and United Way. Program development has long been an interest of Dr. Oliver. She has successfully founded community-based programs in Washington, Idaho and Rhode Island.

Dr. Oliver is currently in private practice in the state of Idaho.

Lorry Roberts

"There is no greater responsibility in the world than being a human being."

At age seventy-three, in the year 2000, I am the youngest of six children. My only surviving sibling, a ninety-three year old sister, lives in Nebraska, where we grew up on a farm near Hastings.

As a child, I rode over two miles to parochial school in a "bunk," a small covered wagon pulled by a horse. Mother heated bricks to keep our feet warm while riding to school. I had two brothers and one sister, all old enough to be my parents. We lost the farm in 1934, but due to President Roosevelt's intervention for farmers, we were able to stay on the place and pay rent to the Federal Land Bank. This was a traumatic time in the lives of these proud, independent people. I remember how humiliated my parents were when they had to apply for government "relief" to receive coal, clothes and bedding.

Two older brothers nearer my age were drafted into the military in 1942 and were gone for four years. Meanwhile, Mother, Dad (age seventy) and I worked hard trying to run the farm. We milked cows and farmed 160 acres using horses, but it was impossible to maintain it all. We left the farm and moved to the little town of Roseland, where I went to high school. I was the only one of our family of six who graduated. I had a wonderful, close relationship with my father. I don't remember my parents ever hugging me and though they were undemonstrative, I knew they loved me. They were always proud of my accomplishments. When I was valedictorian, the principal came back behind stage and said, "We had better get this show on the road because there is a guy out there who is going to bust every button on his vest," and *that guy* was my father. We silently walked the field together for hours, feeling warm and comfortable, just spending time together.

I earned a college scholarship but decided to work for the Telephone Company for three years. I had an opportunity to learn the long distance board or go to Harvard Air Force Base to learn the PBX Board. At that time, the base sounded appealing. This was a good move for me because learning the PBX Board was the experience I needed to start my Simplot career.

I married and in less than four years, by the time I was 24, we had three babies; Kathy, Toni and Dee. I didn't have to leave home to work but by taking in laundry and picking fruit, I was able to help out with the bills.

When my youngest started first grade, I realized that if I didn't go to work, we probably wouldn't be able to educate them. My PBX Board experience landed me a job at the Simplot Food Division in Caldwell. I was hired and I worked evenings for over three years. I missed having dinner with the family but the girls learned to cook and iron at an early age.

In 1961, the company bought a small printing press to put out a newsletter for the Caldwell plant Food Division and I was able to transfer. When the man who was operating the press left, the company was going to hire another printer but they didn't want to pay union wage. I went to Leon Jones, president of the Food Division and told him that I could run that machine. Well, I knew how to turn it on and how to clean it. I made a lot of adjustments at two in the morning with an instruction book in one hand and a screwdriver in the other. We got busier all of the time, which led to an expansion to all food division plants and a corporate managerial position in a new Boise office with twenty-two employees.

I designed a new logo in the late 1970s that is currently in use; my legacy at the J.R. Simplot Company. Any time you can learn on the job, you can't lose. I worked at Simplot Company for over twenty-eight years and was the first woman supervisor, manager and corporate photographer.

I was offered an early retirement to downsize management in 1987.

Following retirement, I grabbed my backpack and went to Europe, where I met lots of people and saw a lot of beautiful country.

I can't say I ever really retired, because I started my own publishing company, Legendary Publishing, and managed this business for twelve years. In April 2000, I sold Legendary Publishing and started my third career, Book Lore Publications, where I will continue teaching publishing classes at Boise State University, consulting with clients who want to write family history, poetry, children's stories or family recipes. I assist them in making this dream come true with the new revolutionary

books-on-demand printing. I love to see the look on the faces of authors when I put "their" book in their hands.

I have been a Soroptimist for 33 years and love it now as much as when I joined. I was Caldwell Club president and treasurer, worked in Growth and Development and on the Nomination Committee at the Federation level, and then at the International level as Coordinator for International Goodwill and Understanding. I am currently appointed to two additional years as Soroptimist International Liaison for Project Five-O.

The International Goodwill and Understanding is special because it encompasses many things, including the refugees and their problems. Understanding is what we must word harder at because our world is shrinking. We must understand and learn to look at other people's side of the story.

Keeping a positive attitude in life is important. When I work with young girls in journal class, I tell them that positive attitude makes life better for you and people around you. There have been a lot of upbeat people in my life and I love to laugh.

I started cross-country skiing at age fifty and the beautiful sights revived my soul. Exercise is important to me. I love to walk and I am active in the Senior Olympics, where I have won several medals due to my competitive nature.

I love teaching the class "Fabulous Living After Fifty," the best time of your life. You have the whole world to look forward to. Keep active, eat healthy, and watch your weight. You can be a grumpy, beat-up person in a nursing home or you can be active until the end. I taught this class at Boise State University and for the Blind and Visually Impaired.

I have fun being "Charlie Chaplin." We all have a child within us; Charlie does this for me. I have won great prizes imitating Charlie at conventions, nursing homes and parties.

A loving person must be one who recognizes responsibility. There is no greater responsibility in the world than being a human being, believe it.

Lorry has received numerous humanitarian awards for her life-long devotion to helping people around the world through her teaching, mentoring and volunteerism. Her most recent award is Who's Who in Executives and Businesses.

Independence I have long considered the grand blessing of life, the basis of every virtue...

— Mary Wollstonecraft

Marge Formo

"I was the only girl in my science and math classes."

Marge was born in the large city of Schenectady, New York, in 1920. She was a tomboy and loved to join in all the sports boys played. She is close to her brothers and sisters and has pleasant memories of all the family times: swimming, playing and picnicking.

"Dad lost our home and business due to the Depression era. He never recuperated from the losses. We were poor in my youth so I worked taking care of children, and then turned the money over to my parents. My aunt loaned me money for school, which I paid back when I graduated." While in school, Marge had a penchant for science and advanced math and she found that she was the only girl in these classes. She cherishes having her grandmother's diplomas in her possession, along with her own.

"In 1942, I started with a career in nursing, which ultimately put our children through school. A year later, I joined the Army Nurse Corps, at which time I went to Europe. During the war, I supervised the septic surgery area in the hospital where I took care of injured soldiers and servicemen.

"When I returned home, I entered the University of Minnesota where I studied to become a hospital administrator. I met Harlan Formo there and we were married for twenty years. We have three children: Richard, Douglas and Susan. It was a shock when he died suddenly while we were camping. Looking back, I regret not taking trips with him. After his death, I went back to work as a Nurse Administrator in the Boise school system and I've lived here for forty-three years.

"I've always wanted to contribute. My caring nature and wanting to help people led me to my career and to volunteerism. When I volunteer at the hospital, it's only the patients I want to work with. This gives me satisfaction and fulfillment. I'm an active volunteer at St. Luke's Hospital, a member of Soroptimist International of Boise, where I've participated for twenty-nine years, and I belong to the P.E.O., an international organization for women. I was one of the board members for Community Guardian for ten years. This organization is appointed by the Ada County Commissioners. We regularly visit clients for whom we have been appointed guardians to assure they have caring visitors and that their needs are fulfilled.

"I believe that keeping a positive attitude, staying upbeat, being yourself and doing the best you can is the way to find happiness and success. Choose something you like to do for otherwise, you will never be successful at your endeavors."

Marge's hobbies include reading, knitting, swimming, bridge and singing in the church choir. She plans to move to Coeur d'Alene, Idaho, to be near her family.

Francelle Fritz

"It is important for me to stay healthy and self-sufficient."

I was born in Cedar City, Utah, on February 4, 1923.

My mother came to Cedar City in 1910. She came from Wisconsin to teach school. Soon after she arrived, she met my father. They were married months later. During the Depression, my father was out of work. He did odd jobs such as shearing sheep. I remember my parents sending the wool to the Barren Woolen Mills in Portland, Oregon, where the wool was made into blankets. I still have a few of the soft comforters.

In the fall of 1942 when I was enrolled at Utah State, I decided to enlist in the WAVES. I had to be twenty years old to enlist. So in April of 1943, I enlisted. I moved to New York and began attending classes at Hunter College in New York City. I was only there for six weeks when the Navy sent me to Milledgeville, Georgia, to attend Storekeeper's school. I was there through the insufferable heat of the summer of 1943. But I got a break from the southern humidity when I was shipped over to Hawaii with the first contingent of WAVES to be sent overseas. I was stationed at Kahului, Maui, until the war ended and I was discharged in December 1945.

Upon arrival back in the States, I began employment at the Union Pacific Lodge on the North Rim of the Grand Canyon. It was at the lodge that I met my future husband. We both accepted employment at the Sun Valley Lodge in the fall of 1947 and, in May 1948, we were married. We lived in Sun Valley for several years before moving to Boise in 1955. Together, we have eight children and I chose to stay at home to raise each one. I also continued my involvement in church and school all through the children's growing years.

The children attended parochial schools all thirteen years of education. Each child has worked his/her way through college and graduated. All of my children have received a Master's Degree, three in Education and one in Social Work. I have a daughter living in the Basque Country in Spain where she teaches English. I have had the opportunity to visit her and her family on two occasions. She has two children who speak English, Spanish and Basque.

At present, I belong to a senior group at my church, WAVES Veterans, and Life Care Auxiliary. It is important for me to stay healthy and self-sufficient.

I have been blessed with a close family, for which I am continually grateful.

Carol Dick

"No matter what we decide to do, we should do it well and give it all that we can. It's the best reward we can give ourselves."

I was born in Cambridge, Idaho in 1933 to Ellis and Bessie Peterson. I am the eldest of four children. I have two sisters and one brother.

I grew up in Cambridge and graduated from Cambridge High School. We lived on a little farm and the folks owned a grocery store. When Dad sold the store, he sold the farm and bought a lumberyard. We all learned to work hard at an early age.

When World War II started, Dad didn't qualify for the draft so we stayed at home to support the war effort. We took our dimes and quarters to school each week to pay for Saving's Stamps, which were accumulated in booklets until their were enough to buy a U.S. Saving's Bond. During those years, patriotism was a large part of everyone and I feel that this is something missing from most people today.

My folks always stressed to us that we could do anything we wanted, as long as we worked hard to meet our goals. That is why I have always felt that I could do whatever I wanted and be whatever I wanted to be. Just tell me that I can't do something and I'll prove you wrong. One of my favorite sayings is, "Anything you can do, I can do better."

In my junior year of high school, I met my husband Garold, the love of my life. The following year on August 1, 1951, we were married. Ten days later he left for Korea. He was gone for one year. While Gerald was gone, I went to business school. I then worked for Attorney Gilbert Norris who later became a District Court Judge. When Gerald was discharged, he returned home and we moved to Weiser, Idaho. We bought a farm and started our family. Within a few years we had three sons, Michael, Douglas and Gary.

In 1964, I started to work in the Assessor's office in Washington County as a temporary clerk. This was the beginning of my life in politics. As time passed, I substituted for a friend as a Roll Clerk. This involved putting the Assessment rolls together and taking care of all the records. I remember many nights going home from the office frustrated over the busy day. My husband would ask me if I was ready to run for Assessor and I'd tell him that I wouldn't have the job if they gave it to me. But soon that became a reality and I was asked to run for the position. It took a lot of persuasion, but I decided to give it a try. Campaigning is hard work and it is not easy for me to ask others for help when I am the one who enjoys helping those around me.

I was elected to the position in 1970 to a four-year term. That is when I was really put to the test as the first woman elected as Assessor in Washington County. I had to face doing a job that had always been done by a man. It was difficult but it was done.

I was elected President of the Assessors Association and served as Chairman of the Legislation Commission. In 1974, I was reelected Assessor. In 1977, I was asked for permission to submit my name to the

Governor as a candidate for State Tax Commissioner. This was the second biggest decision for me but with the support and encouragement of my husband and boys, I said that I would do it.

A few months later while serving on a Governors Commission on Local Government, I was contacted and informed that I had been selected as the first woman Tax Commissioner for the State of Idaho. What a challenge this was. I had to start over but I had a lot of good support.

While I was Assessor and Legislative Chairman for the Assessors Association, Morgan Munger, a past Commissioner from Gem County and a current Legislator I had known and respected for several years, became a very cherished mentor. I worked closely with him on a number of legislative bills. After I became Tax Commissioner, we continued to work together on legislation and state issues. A few years later, Morgan also was appointed a Tax Commissioner, so we were able to continue to work together for the good of the state. After Morgan's retirement and later his untimely death, I was left with a large void in my life. He had been there to support and encourage me for many years.

I have gone on to serve on the Board of the National Association of Tax Administrators. This entitled me to travel several times to Washington D.C. for meetings to promote state needs. This was an extra bonus above and beyond my job, which enabled me to attempt to make a difference. I believe that everyone wants to make a difference, even if it is in a very small way. I was fortunate to be able to work at a job I liked, a job that was a real challenge and also one that helps the people.

When we start out young and try a lot of different jobs, it helps to determine the areas we like and the ones we do not. It also gives us a chance to grow. Everyone is different and we don't all fit the same mold. We just have to find our own niche. But no matter what we decide to do, we should always do it well and give it all that we can. It's the best reward we can give ourselves.

I am now the grandmother of five super grandchildren. I retired from the Tax Commissioner's office in 1991 and moved back to Weiser where I could be close to my family. My daughter-in-law and I shared the ownership of a flower shop, The Blossom Shop, which I sold three years ago.

During three months of the cold Idaho winters, my husband Gerald and I travel to the warmth of the Arizona desert. But we always return to family and business in Weiser.

If I had my life to live over, I'm not sure that I would make any changes. I have a wonderful husband, family and friends who have always supported me completely.

I have learned that nothing ever comes free or easy. You have to work hard for what you want. If it's important to you, then all the sacrifice and work is worth it. The respect and friendship you receive makes it all worthwhile.

Calla Cornwell

"I have a wonderful network of friends I have made over the years. It gives me great joy to stay in touch with special friends."

My paternal grandparents emigrated from Sweden in 1889. They lived one winter in a sod house near Hooper, Nebraska. They had little to eat except coffee and bread. To keep warm they twisted wild hay to burn. My father grew up in a loving home with kind parents, two older brothers and five sisters. He experienced a feeling of warmth and belonging that few know today.

My maternal grandmother was born in Ridgeville, Indiana, in 1883. Her father had traced his ancestors back to the coming of the Mayflower. At age one year, she and her parents moved from Indiana to Nebraska in a covered wagon. She and my grandfather were married in 1904 in Nebraska and they moved to South Dakota when my mother was three years old.

My grandparents' one goal in life was to see that all four of their children received a high school education. Each of them did and attended one year of college in order to obtain teaching certificates. And then, one by one, they began careers teaching in the area. My mother's greatest joy was helping her grandchildren with their schoolwork. She and my father were wonderful, loving, caring parents and grandparents.

I was born on April 24, 1932, in South Dakota. My father farmed and the Depression years were difficult. Then the drought hit and, in 1941, my parents moved to Oregon. We lived in Portland during the war years. I remember sitting in the living room listening to the announcement of the attack on Pearl Harbor.

I remember the black curtains over the windows so no light would show. I remember gasoline rationing and food rationing cards. I also remember when the end of the war was announced.

In 1946, my father's health was not good from the years of working in a galvanizing plant and the doctor advised that my parents go back on the farm. They found a small piece of acreage they could afford in Caldwell, Idaho. I was in high school at the time.

After graduation, college was not in my plans so I began my working years in an office in Caldwell. It was the General Office for the Idaho Department Stores. I was married in September 1950 and continued to work until my first child was born in 1953. I was at home for the next twelve years. Financially, I needed to work again so I went back to the same company part time, which very soon became full time.

That was the beginning of the computer era. I loved to run any kind of machine and at that time keypunched cards and computers were beginning to take off. We moved to Boise in 1965 and I began working in the computer department of Mountain States Wholesale and worked my way up to supervisor. During those years I took some night classes at Boise State.

My next career move was with MacGregor Triangle Construction Company as an accountant. Next, I chose to work for Boise Building

Supply in accounting and computers. Boise Cascade bought the company in 1978. I continued my career with Boise Cascade until my retirement in 1991. I worked for the building supply division and, during the last nine years, I managed the office for their in-house print shop.

I became involved in the many volunteer projects that Boise Cascade supported. My favorite was dressing dolls and bears for the Salvation Army, which we collected for the Christmas Toy drive. I coordinated this project for several years.

I divorced in 1973 and remarried in 1974. My four children (three daughters and a son) all live in the valley, as do my seven grandchildren and two great grandchildren.

After retirement, my husband and I took up the frustrating game of golf and now live near Purple Sage Golf Course in Caldwell. I stay active through my church and volunteer time to work part time in the office.

I enjoy reading and Caldwell has a wonderful library. I spend several hours there each week. I also enjoy taking naps, spoiling our twelve-year old Manx cat and visiting with friends and family.

I have belonged to several organizations. When my children were young I was active in the Mother's Club of First Christian Church. After I returned to work I belonged to Credit Woman's International and served as secretary and treasurer.

My favorite organization was The In Plant Printing Management Association Idaho Chapter. I was active in it for nine years. It was small but made a big impact on the community and the business world.

If I could do something different with my life it would be to have spent more quality time with my children as they were growing.

I have a wonderful network of friends that I have made over the years. It gives me great joy to stay in touch with special friends.

Sally Baker

The most important tool we need, doesn't cost a dime.
It is the ability to laugh at ourselves.

When I was a teenager, I could pick up any magazine or newspaper and find articles about what to expect of that part of my life. The ups and downs emotionally; the conflicts with authority. There were health classes in school dealing with puberty. Certainly the library shelves were crowded with books on dealing with and/or being a pre-teen or teen.

When I married, friends gave me books on young love; the newlyweds; living in harness with another; the abyss of an unbalanced checkbook.

Then as I began a career, once again there was an abundance of periodicals with endless articles addressed to the working woman. Those that dealt with upward mobility; being mentored; sexual harassment; sexual freedom; recognizing opportunities; the glass ceiling, et cetera.

But when I turned 50, I looked around for information to help me deal with some of the things I was experiencing and found very little. My body was changing. I had a hysterectomy. The employment picture was tilting toward younger people. Everybody agreed that it was nice that you had 20 years experience but would prefer that you no be over 30 years old. Even an Irishman found that tough to achieve.

Suddenly, you're talking to your children about things you used to discuss with your peers. The morality of the world exploded into cheap shots between generations. I heard the same comments from many colleagues of my generation.

Since there are so many of us in this brand new world of 50 and over, I began compiling research to provide the same kind of information that those before me compiled for those who were sweet sixteen.

Misery loves company, so settle back and discover that you are not alone; there are millions of us going through the same thing. The most important tool we need, doesn't cost a dime. It is the ability to laugh at ourselves. Recognize that every problem has several solutions. The purpose of [my] book is to help you regain your confidence and take charge of your life and future. Change your mind; change your life. So let's get at it. You are a work of art and it is time that you know it!

— *Excerpted from the Introduction of Sally Baker's new book-in-progress,* I'm Too Damn Young to Be This Old

Ona Healy

"...but we thought we were rich..."

I was born in St. Louis, Missouri, in November of 1931. This was during the Depression and shortly after my birth, my father lost his job. Since my mother was not well and unable to care for me alone, my father carried me around with him while he looked for a job. He eventually began working at the General Motors factory.

I began kindergarten in St. Louis and continued there until the second grade. It was during this time that we began to attend Sunday school. There I learned to recite the books of the Bible and realized that Christ died for me and I accepted Him into my life. This was a decision that affected the rest of my life.

We then moved to the little town of Florissant, where I attended a two-room school. Due to crowded conditions, they taught the fifth through seventh grades one year and then fifth, sixth and eighth grades the next. When I was in the sixth grade, I realized that I would be skipping the next year and going to the eighth. This was a challenge for me but since I did so well without the seventh grade, my teacher gave me all the requirements during the summer months and I was able to complete them all to graduate. I was very excited to go on to high school.

I attended Riverview High, which meant riding the school bus for many miles. The older boys delighted in harassing the younger boys. It was a very noisy and sometimes frightening trip each way. During school, I worked on the school newspaper and sang in the choir. Both of these activities prepared me for my adult life.

Shortly after graduation, my parents decided to move to Idaho, since my father no longer wanted to work for General Motors. My uncle, who lived in Emmett, found a small farm near Nampa and arranged the purchase for my father. My father bought a two-ton truck and we loaded it with most of our belongings and started out for Idaho. Our home in Florissant had not sold so my mother and youngest brother had to stay behind until it did. It was an interesting trip to Idaho. We traveled as far each day as we could, my sister and I singing at night to keep our father awake until he finally decided to stop for the night. We then camped out in the truck and cooked meals on a camp stove.

When we arrived at the farmhouse, we really had our work cut out for us. The house required many hours of hard labor to make it clean enough for us to want to live there, especially the kitchen area. We soon found out the land was not productive so my father had to resort to trimming trees.

Our neighbors informed us that they attended church in Notus, so we went there as well. One Sunday, I was sitting in front of a young man who had a great voice — little did I know that he was to become my husband. After a short courtship of eight months, we were married.

We made our home in Boise, where we both had full-time jobs. Wages back in the 1950s were not too great, but we thought we were rich since we both came from homes that were very frugal and where you learned to get by on what you earned. Ray worked for a grocery store and I worked for an insurance company.

We were married for five-and-a-half years before we started a family. Our first son was born in November of 1955; our next child, a girl, was born two years later. We were so delighted to have two lively children but God had other plans for us. We moved to our present home in April of 1959 and had another daughter the following year. Two years later, we had our youngest son.

Our children grew up going to the same schools, going to church, playing in the band at Borah, making good friends, and they were a joy to us. We now enjoy being together as much as possible. We have ten grandchildren, the oldest being 21 and the youngest being 14. It may be soon that some of them will marry and we look forward to great-grandchildren in the future.

We recently celebrated our 50th wedding anniversary. Our children, especially our daughter who lives in Boise, worked really hard to make it a special occasion for us. After fifty years of marriage, we are still very much in love. We credit God for this and thank Him each day for His blessings.

Sylvia Creek

"In 1930, we bought a new Ford Coupe with a rumble seat. We paid $700 cash. Now we were living."

I was born April 15, 1906, in Eaton, Colorado. My mother was Elizabeth Ellen Overley and my father, Simeon Titmus. Daddy died in Greeley, Colorado, in 1932. He is buried in the Greeley Cemetery.

I can still remember when I was three and had bronchial pneumonia. The doctor came to the house and insisted I take a spoonful of castor oil. I remember him and Mother standing over my bed holding the teaspoon over my head. My brother Loren held my feet while Mother held my arms and Dr. Loren forced the awful tasting oil down my throat.

My parents were divorced in 1910. In 1911, Mother was asked to come to Boise. A friend of Mother's, Mrs. Sharp, wrote to Mom and asked if she would like to come to Idaho, cook for twenty men and live at the Boise Butcher Shop on Madison Street for $20 a month. Mom wired her to send money for train tickets for my brother Roy, Mom and me. We arrived in Boise on May 25, 1911.

We lived in a small room in the back of the butcher shop for about a year and then moved in with my brother Loren and his wife Gladys who had moved to Boise when we did. My mother left the butcher shop and became a cook for the William Davidson family on Warm Springs Avenue and then for the Hoover Family on Harrison Boulevard.

Mother married Hubert Matthews in May 1915 in Vale, Oregon. Bert worked at the butcher shop and had a house outside the gate. We lived there for ten years. I went to school through the eighth grade at Park School then to Boise High for four years. After high school, I continued my education at Links Business College for six weeks, just long enough for the school to place me in a job.

I was hired at the Idaho Laundry. My starting wage was $20 a week. In three months my pay was raised to $25 a week. Then I was rich.

In late 1927, I went on a double date with a boy and his friend (Charlie) and my friend Louise. Charlie and I hit it off that evening and began dating for one and one half years. We were married on August 3, 1929.

We moved into the Zurcher Apartments, which still remain. We paid $30 a month for rent. Charlie worked at the telephone company and earned extra money by playing in the band at the Bucket of Blood dance hall at 13th and Main Street. I continued to work at the Laundry, then quit to work at Baker Supply for $100 a month.

In 1930, we bought a new Ford coupe with a rumble seat. We paid $ 700 cash for it. Now we were living.

Our first child (a daughter) was stillborn on June 25, 1932. We named her Carol Ann. She is buried at Morris Hill Cemetery.

I remember one Sunday morning, I wanted to roast a chicken and the chicken legs stuck up so high that I couldn't keep the roaster lid on so I put a can of peas on top to hold it down. Charlie was asleep so I walked down the alley to Mom's to visit for a while. When I returned the kitchen was a mess, the oven door had blown off and was laying on the floor; the chicken and peas were plastered all over the ceiling and walls. The can of peas had exploded. The lesson I learned from this was don't ever put a sealed can of food into a hot oven.

Our son Larry was born in 1934. Dennis was born in 1939. And Dean was born in 1944. Our family was complete and the boys were a handful, but a handful of joy as well.

Charlie retired in 1975 and we began to travel. We bought an eighteen-foot trailer and cruised across the United States. We began to venture off into the Arizona desert each winter. We did that for almost twenty years. But Charlie became sick and for the last three trips to Arizona, and he spent most of his time in bed. In 1995, we decided that we should stay home for the winter. Charlie passed away in his sleep on May 20, 1995.

It is lonely without him. We always played cards for two to three hours each day. And every night we would have a drink. He loved Hot Buttered Rum and Hot Brandy. Sometimes we drank beer while playing cards. We would bet on our games, usually a quarter on Gin Rummy. We played Gin, Honeymoon Bridge, Casino, Kings on the Corner and once in a while Checkers. We wagered one dollar on Honeymoon Bridge.

I am now ninety years old and live in a mobile home park. I enjoy all the people at the park. We play cards twice a week, Bingo on Wednesday night, have a pancake breakfast once a month and occasionally a block party is thrown.

Thank God I am still enjoying life.

No good deed goes unpunished.

— Clare Boothe Luce

Delores Crow

"You only fail if you don't try again."

Delores Crow was born in 1931 in Clovis, New Mexico, across the border from where her parents lived in West Texas. "We lived in a big white farm house with a huge porch. There was a grain silo and a big barn with little kittens running around." Her family moved to Jerome, Idaho, four years after she was born. "It was the Depression and nothing would grow in the dustbowl down there." Her father was a farmer, but he moved to Idaho to be a carpenter.

In her household, being good meant being good. The youngest of five daughters, Delores was the most spoiled; the only chore she did was to keep her room straightened up. She attended first grade through high school in Jerome. She thought her second grade teacher, Mrs. Redford, "was gorgeous. She may not have been, but I thought she was." After high school, Delores went to a Salt Lake City business school where she met Wayne, of Wendell, Idaho. "I married him for all the wrong reasons and because he was the only man who could put up with me." They tried for many years to have children but after three of them died (born prematurely by five or six months) they decided to adopt. Just as the paperwork was about to go through, they conceived and had their first child, "and we never stopped." Ultimately, Wayne and Delores had three boys and three girls.

In 1965, Delores entered the Mrs. Idaho Pageant. She was already a wife and mother at this time. The area entrance exam was written, which she passed. She went to Pocatello for the finals, having no idea what was expected of her. When she arrived, she knew there was going to be a question/answer period but she learned that she would also have to arrange a children's birthday party. "I went to what was the equivalent of a dollar store and bought all the stuff the night before, and got it all set up." She was then told she would have to narrate the party. "I remember someone talking but I was in so much shock I didn't know it was me." Needless to say, she was first runner-up, an experience that gave her a lot of confidence in herself.

It was her husband who turned Delores on to politics. She worked with him in an accounting practice, Crow & Associates, for many years. While both dabbled in politics at first, they soon became engrossed with it. Delores had left town for two years and when she returned, she was not on the list of candidates. The following election season, she was the front-runner, received the nomination and was elected. During her stay in the Legislature, she has been on the Joint Finance and Appropriations Committee and has served as Chair of the Environmental Affairs Committee. She currently serves as Chair of the Revenue and Taxation Committee.

"There was no particular gender bias in the Legislature. I can count on one hand the number of times it may have been a factor." Delores has one more word of advice to all the naysayers of politics. "I may be a politician but I am also a person — I am a woman, wife, mother and grandmother. That is what everyone needs to remember — even the President, and celebrities as well are human beings."

"You only fail if you don't try again," she says, a personal philosophy which has carried her through her life. She has no regrets; when her husband had cancer ("he was never sick"), finally passing away after nine years, she never felt as though there was something she should have said, something she shouldn't have done. "I'm very lucky in that respect."

When the stresses of political office become too much and she decides to step down, Delores plans nothing more than to live and be healthy, though she may not have to work at that very hard. "People in my family have a tendency to live long." Her daughter encourages her to do healthy things and Delores has many hobbies; she has a lot of bird feeders around the house, but she has no time to get out into the wild and watch them; she likes spectator sports and gardening. She says, "I like the girl stuff but I also like the guy stuff." Her activities in the community include "everything to do with children, many animal programs and the Welcome Wagon, when that was a big thing."

The older woman's love is not love of herself, nor of herself mirrored in a lover's eyes, nor is it corrupted by need. It is a feeling of tenderness so still and deep and warm that it gilds every grass blade and blesses every fly. It includes the ones who have a claim on it, and a great deal else besides. I wouldn't have missed it for the world.

— Germaine Greer

Loretta Reed

"Don't fight against it, accept what comes, turn it over to the Lord and move on."

I was born on a farm in Adrian, Oregon, on December 14, 1933. I was the middle child in a happy, loving and Christian family. My brother Bill is thirteen months older and my sister Lorraine is two-and-one-half years younger.

When I was three years old, my family moved to Phillipsburg, Kansas, so that my father could take over the family farm. Soon the drought years began and it became difficult to make a living on the Kansas farm. I remember the masses of grasshoppers, tornado warnings, and storm cellars. I vividly remember watching a tornado approach as we climbed into the dark cellar. I remember the spiders, the musty smell and the anxiety as we waited in the cellar for the storm to pass. I remember wondering if the black cloud would continue coming toward our house, and if the house would be standing when we opened the cellar door.

My family returned to Oregon when I was seven years old. We settled on a farm near my birthplace. I learned at an early age about teamwork and responsibility. On the farm we shared the chores and duties of the day. My brother and I would get up early and feed and care for our own cow. During my teen years, one of my chores was hoeing beets during the summer, which I detested. But it did encourage me to get more education and make sure that I had a career.

I was an independent child. When I was ten years old my parents had to take my sister into Caldwell for emergency surgery. While they were gone, I realized that the cows needed to be milked. I brought them in from the field, hooked up the milking machines and milked all of them. Then I separated the cream from the milk. The process was complete upon my parents' arrival home.

I graduated from Adrian High School at the age of seventeen. I began college in 1951 at Bob Jones University in South Carolina. But after two years of school I wanted to earn my own money and decided that a career was more important than a degree. I got a job at Idaho Power in Payette, Idaho. One of my duties was to pick up the mail. It was at the Payette Post Office where I met Richard Reed, an apprentice mortician with the local funeral home. It was his job, too, to pick up the mail. After a whirlwind romance, we were married in 1954.

Richard and I moved to American Falls in 1955 where our first daughter was born. Soon we moved to Nampa, Idaho, where Richard was employed at the Alsip Funeral Home. Shortly after the move, our second daughter was born. Then soon after her birth, I began to hemorrhage and only an emergency hysterectomy saved me. It was at this time that my faith was strengthened and I developed the philosophy, 'Don't fight against it, accept what comes, turn it over to the Lord and move on.' And that's what I did.

I spent the next seven years of my life as a homemaker and community volunteer. When our younger daughter was seven, I decided it was time for me to get a job and begin a career. I began working as a clerical typist for the Idaho Personnel Commission and enrolled in night courses in Personnel Administration and Public Administration at Boise State University.

I worked my way up at the Commission and was with them for thirty years. I worked as a Classifications and Test Development Analyst. And for a period of time I worked as Special Assistant to the Director.

After retiring in 1997, I enjoyed two years of travel and volunteering. I was then asked to return to work *temporarily* to assist the Department of Juvenile Corrections. I have been working part-time since the return.

I continue to enjoy all the pleasures of life, especially family. It is a thrill to be a part of my grandchildren's accomplishments. I pray that each will be fortunate enough to embrace the faith, drive, and optimistic spirit of their grandmother as they continue their own life adventures.

The state of the world today
demands that women become less modest
and dream/plan/act/risk on a larger scale.

— Charlotte Bunch

Jean Wilson

"I hope to celebrate my seventy-fifth birthday rafting down one of Idaho's scenic rivers."

A large family was considered normal when I married in 1947. We planned for twelve. Thank God we stopped at five. All of my children are alive and a great support to me. I have two sons and three daughters, ages fifty-two to forty-five. I have six grandchildren, three boys and three girls, ages thirty-one to eighteen. As of the year 2000, there are three great-grandchildren. My husband died in 1962 and, sadly, he missed all of the joy of being a grandparent.

In the winter of 1962, I began working at The Book Shop as a part-time employee. Nancy Stringfellow was my mentor and she convinced me to become a full-time salesperson. I was thrilled because not only did I love to read, I loved the retail business. In 1946, I had worked in specialty stores on Fifth Avenue in New York City. Learning the scope of The Book Shop, meeting authors, and helping the store become the focal point for Idaho material was a joy. Nancy retired in 1970 and I became the manager. In 1972, I was elected to the American Booksellers Association Board of Directors. I served for eight years, one as Vice President and one as Secretary.

In 1978, I was chosen to be part of a trade commission to the United Kingdom. Twenty book industry delegates from America spent two weeks in London and Oxford meeting with our counterparts in England. It was an amazing experience. As there were only two women delegates we had to be very effective and vocal. All of us learned much about the International Book Business.

There are no roadblocks for me. I am a Leo and it never occurred to me that I wouldn't do well in the book business. In 1973, I had purchased fifty percent of the shares in The Book Shop and I finalized buying all the remaining shares in 1982. It was a good decision and I have never regretted it. One of my sons now owns the store and another son works there.

I was a child in the 1920s and 30s. As an Idaho woman born and bred, I was lucky during the depression. My mother was from a ranching family and could stretch a dollar. After my father lost his cattle business, we worked for Swift and Company. We were poor but there was always food on the table and nickels for ice cream. The North End of Boise was a great place to grow. There were lots of children and working dads and stay-at-home moms.

During this time, Boise had some fine parades and celebrations. Music week was held in front of the Capitol and we sat on the hard cement steps, enchanted. The Natatorium was still in operation. We could catch the bus, another nickel, and swim all day. We played lots of sandlot ball, made paper dolls, played dress-up, rode bicycles in vacant lots and played Ping-Pong in the Mayor's garage. And sometimes we skated to Hyde Park for the five-cent ice cream cone.

We got through the Depression. Our parents sacrificed a lot so that we could have some fun. Then in 1941, my mother died and there were a lot of changes. My father traveled so my sisters and I moved into an apartment. I was fourteen and my sisters were twenty-one and nineteen. We worked and pooled our money and learned how to cope without the mainstay in our lives. My job was record girl at the Music Center on Main Street.

Boise changed forever, as did the United States, when Pearl Harbor was attacked. Two air bases were established, Gowen Field and Mountain Home. Enlistment of my sisters' friends, the attack on Wake Island, B-17's constantly overhead, the influx of men and women from all parts of America certainly made all of us conscious that a war was going on. I was in high school, wrapped up in my own interests, but I was aware of the changes in Boise.

I loved high school. I loved my classes, especially English and Drama. I learned to manage my time, stay active in Drama, ROTC, the Minute Maids, and my job after school. I grew up very quickly, but I am pleased with the results. I learned patience, strength, and commitment during those turbulent years.

After two years at Boise Junior College, I left Boise to live in New York City. My sister had married a New Yorker and they invited me to live with them. My dad shed tears when I left but not me. It was an adventure and it lasted a year. Every day was an eye opener. I got the job on Fifth Avenue. I managed the first floor where the staff consisted of eighteen girls. I was bossy even at nineteen. And no one ever got it straight in their mind that I was from Idaho not Ohio.

In 1947 I was married to Willard A. Wilson, an Idaho boy who became the first children's dentist in the state, but the Korean War split us apart. Willard was back in the service three months after we married. He was stationed at a MASH unit on the 39th Parallel. I was pregnant when he departed. He returned in eighteen months and we moved to Fort Lewis, Washington, for six months. We had to readjust to each other, the Army life and a family. But we survived, and moved back to Boise. We were thrilled.

After a career in the Book business I continue to love to read, garden, and to bake cookies. I also love to give book talks and write book reviews. But most importantly, I love being with family and friends, discussing books, health, state of the union, sports events and how the superstores are ruining our nation. I have few regrets. I have experienced too many losses to worry much about what might have been. I feel blessed that Idaho is my family's home and that I grew up in a community that is full of love and beauty.

I am seventy-three and hope to celebrate my seventy-fifth birthday rafting down one of Idaho's scenic rivers. I am Idaho born and bred, independent, opinionated, and a survivor.

Lucille Irwin Smylie

"I've met people from all walks of life and have found them to be generally good and kind by nature."

I grew up on a modest farm in Oklahoma. Oh, we had a tennis court and quite a bit of land, but we were by no means wealthy. With seven brothers and sisters, my parents couldn't really afford to send me to a four-year college during the Depression so I went to the local business college for two years.

After graduation, I joined my older sister who was working in Washington, D.C. I worked in a law firm there for several years when D. Worth Clark, a Congressman from Pocatello, Idaho, introduced me to my future husband, Robert Smylie. Bob was a law student at George Washington University and worked in the same law firm where I worked.

When the war started, I had the opportunity to go to Rio de Janeiro to work for the State Department. It was an exciting place to live for a young lady! I lived there for about eighteen months while Bob was in the service. Bob and I got married in New York after I returned, and then moved to Philadelphia, where Bob was stationed. He was eventually shipped off to the Philippines, while I worked for a judge in

California for the duration of the war.

In 1946, Bob was finally released from the service and we moved back to Washington, D.C., for a short while. Bob was then offered a position with the new Attorney General from Idaho, Robert Ailshie. We had visited Bob's family in Caldwell on our way back from California so I already knew I would like the area when we moved to Boise, Idaho, in 1946.

Bob was the assistant to the Attorney General for only a few months before Mr. Ailshie died of a heart attack. Bob was appointed to succeed him and he was subsequently elected to the office. He served as the Attorney General for almost eight years and, after a strenuous campaign, he was elected Governor of Idaho in 1954, a position he would hold for almost twelve years.

We moved into the Governor's Mansion located in Boise. Our two sons, Bill and Steve, were very young. Being the wife of the Governor was both exciting and exhausting as I tried to balance State business and social events with activities that could include the boys. We managed very well, even with the youngest only four years old. The boys must have thought public office was all right as Steve, our youngest, is currently serving in the Idaho House of Representatives.

We always enjoyed the Governors' Conventions, held in a different state each year. There were activities for wives and children of all ages. Perhaps the most exciting time as the wife of the Governor was entertaining delegates from other countries. We entertained groups from both Russia and Japan. Bob and I traveled to Russia in an exchange program, and their delegates came to Boise. This was during the middle of the Cold War but we had the opportunity to get to know these people well, as individuals with families and concerns much like our own.

Being the family-in-residence at the Governor's Mansion had its own adventures. I remember well one time when the local Silver Sage Girl Scout Council asked if it could hold a fundraising tea party at the Mansion. I agreed, as they expected maybe one hundred attendees, and their staff planned to serve everyone themselves. When the day arrived, people came from all over southern Idaho. I guess the opportunity to see the Governor's Mansion was more inviting than we had imagined. Soon we were all out of plates, food and utensils. As the poor Girl Scout staff scrambled to find ways to serve all these people, they ended up going to several of our neighbors, asking to borrow many of the items we lacked. To this day, over fifty years later, people I meet on the street mention that afternoon when they got to come visit the Governor's Mansion for Girl Scout tea.

Overall, I've had a good life with many exciting adventures. I've grown to love the people of Idaho. I've met people from all walks of life and have found them to be generally good and kind by nature. I'm glad to have had the opportunities to travel and meet people from all over the world. Most of all, I am very proud of what Bob has done for the State of Idaho to make it a better place to live.

Ardis Snyder

"I've always believed that a positive attitude prevails for those who possess successful life skills."

Ardis was born and reared in Caldwell, Idaho. At eight years of age, her first paid job was feeding bum, or motherless, lambs with a bottle. She saved her earnings because she had set a goal to use the money for her college education. Ardis always wanted to teach and her first students were her dolls. Her father was instrumental in instilling confidence in Ardis, and encouraged her dream to become a teacher. "He was a wonderful dad, far ahead of other men during his era. He believed in and encouraged me. My brother Cleo also encouraged and counseled me through the years."

"The Depression era came while I was in school and at home, and the hardships caused my parents heartache and difficulty. We raised our own food and meat and this sustained us during a difficult time in history.

"My experiences as a classroom teacher in the Caldwell district were spent as a primary and junior high teacher, where I taught music and English." She quit teaching after meeting her husband. "I married a wonderful man, Jerry Snyder, and we had a daughter named Susan. My husband served four years in World War II, of which twenty-nine months were overseas. He died at a young age, when Susan was only three years old and losing him was extremely hard.

"After my husband's death, I returned to the classroom. Soon after that, a former principal and my mentor, Margaret Stovel, convinced me to be her vice-principal. I basically had what is known today as a three-year internship. Following several years as principal, I was appointed Director of a federally funded project in the Idaho Department of Education. My position involved instituting and supervising the program throughout the state of Idaho. I finished my degrees by attending night and summer school. My mother was a significant help at this time.

"Being actively involved in my community has always been and continues to be an integral part of my life. I joined the Soroptimist International of Boise in 1968. I have held the presidency and other offices and participated in the Ada County Community Guardian program, which is appointed by Ada County Commissioners. We work with nursing home residents (who need that representation) as though they are family and advocate for them.

"I have been active in my church and directed the choir. I've been actively involved with Silver Sage Girl Scout Council and its Executive Board; Past Matron; Eastern Star; Job's Daughters Council; and the Caldwell American Red Cross Board. By invitation, I have membership in two educational organizations, Phi Delta Kappa and Delta Kappa Gamma. I enjoy the challenge of keeping up with the education profession, post-retirement."

"I have always believed that a positive attitude prevails for those who possess successful life skills. I've lived my life believing this has influenced my own life. I've tried to do the best I could day to day, with God's help."

Ardis Snyder is listed in the prestigious book, *Who's Who in American Women.*

FOLLOW WHAT YOU LOVE! Don't deign to ask what "they" are looking for out there. Ask what you have inside. Follow not your interests, which change, but what you are and what you love, which will and should not change.

— Georgie Anne Geyer

Ruby Stone

"She says what she means, she means what she says, and she always follows through."

Ruby is the most senior member of the Idaho State Legislature. She has completed eight sessions and has been reelected for her ninth. But Ruby's life began on February 6, 1924, in Bulloch County, Georgia. Her family lived on a large ranch and grew tobacco and cotton with the help of sharecroppers. She had three older brothers and an older sister who died at eighteen months.

Early memories include her mother cooking Thanksgiving dinner for twenty people (the children eating in a separate room) and her father buying a secondhand Ford that she learned to drive. "I was in hog heaven." She would go into town on Saturday afternoon, go to the movies, and eat ice cream afterwards at the drugstore.

Ruby attended a one-room school that was kind of like kindergarten. Then she transferred to Portal where Mrs. Finch was her first grade teacher. She remembers crying the first day of school because she wanted her mother. Following her graduation from high school, Ruby attended Dickenson's Secretarial and Business school in Kansas City, Missouri. She later took additional classes at Boise State University.

Ruby met Harry Stone, who was in the Air Force, in Savannah, Georgia. A friend told her about this first lieutenant she had met in the officer's club. Four of them went to the beach in Harry's car and on the way home, the car had a flat tire. Ruby got out and helped Harry change the tire. Soon Harry was visiting the family farm and in 1942, they were married.

Ruby and Harry had two children, Diane and Raymond. When Dianne was 11 years old, she was diagnosed with severe diabetes. In her early twenties, she began to lose her eyesight. As a partially sighted person, however, she earned two master's degrees, one in Home Economics/ Human Development, the other in Counseling. She is currently the Administrator of the program for the disabled at the University of Idaho. Raymond, a BSU graduate, lives in Boise.

As an Air Force family, they moved often and Ruby and the family adapted to life in many different places. These included Vanderberg Air Force Base in California and in St. John's, Newfoundland. Her husband was involved in the Atlas missile program and was there when the first missile was fired from the West Coast. In 1960, they came to Boise, Idaho, where Harry was the acting manager of the Mountain Home missile program for American Machine and Foundry until the new manager arrived.

Ruby learned to golf at Vanderberg and has been associated with women's golf as a competitor, administrator and benefactor ever since. She was the first woman to be elected to the Idaho Golf Association Board of Directors, the second woman nationally to be elected to what was basically a men's State Board of Directors. She played a major role in establishing the Junior Girls Golf Program in Idaho. She helped get scholarships for junior girls. In 1993, Ruby Stone was inducted into the Idaho Sports Hall of Fame, only the second woman to be so honored.

Ruby has been involved with politics for many years. She served as an aide to Governor Don Samuelson. She worked as a legislative attaché for fifteen years. Among her positions were secretary to the State Affairs Committee in the House and Journal Clerk in the Senate. She also worked in the Governor's office as manager of the People Programs. She was a major factor in her husband's election to the Idaho House of Representatives. When he died during his first term, Governor John Evans appointed Ruby to complete the term. She has run and been re-elected to the position ever since. Her current Committee assignments are the House State Affairs Committee and, since 1991, Chair of the Local Government Committee.

Ruby has volunteered for many organizations. She has spent over fifty years with youth programs. These include the Cub Scouts, Brownie and Girl Scouts, and the Junior Girls Golf programs. She has been a Red Cross volunteer, Gray Lady and nurse's aide and is a former member the Gowen Field Officers' Wives Club. She has assisted in fund raising for the Heart, Cancer, Diabetes, and Blind Associations. She helped with the Morrison Center Building Committee.

Ruby has a reputation for honesty and integrity and is concerned that this is not being followed in today's political campaigns. She advises people to study the issues, become involved and don't let others speak for you. She says that there is nothing better than to have a reputation for honesty and integrity, and to give of yourself to help others. She advises young people to get all the education they possibly can for that will determine their economic future.

Rachel Tanner

"To keep going, I think we need a dream that we can be in command of."

I was born in Eye Suffolk, England, on July 9, 1922. I was the seventh and youngest child of a country doctor and a clergyman's daughter.

I started school just before my fifth birthday. When I was ten, my father died suddenly. A flu epidemic and overwork was too much for his heart. Our house and lovely garden was sold. My mother and I moved into a wing of my grandparents' home. When I was eleven I was sent off to the same school that my sisters had attended. I was homesick and often bullied. I passed my School Certificate when I was sixteen and left school. Once I had dreamed of being a concert pianist. For a while I considered being a pharmacist but in the end, I chose the library profession. One way to enter the field was to go to a University. The other way was to be an apprentice in a public library and take exams. I chose to do the latter and was offered a job in Ipswich, which was twenty miles from home.

I started working in August 1939. World War II began a few weeks later on September 3 when Hitler marched into Poland. We were now in a world of confusion and fear. We carried our gas masks with us everywhere and put up with food and clothes rationing. A landmine dropped within two miles of the center of town and we could watch dogfights over London or a coastal town in flames. My greatest fear was an invasion, which was happening all throughout Europe. My brother, a submariner was reported to be a prisoner of war after being missing for three months. The fiancé of one of my co-workers was shot down over the English Channel and was killed.

But through it all, I loved working in the library. During the air raids, I studied for the preliminary library exam, which I took and passed the following year.

But I wanted to do more for the war effort. So in December 1941, I began training as a radar technician in London. I didn't have the chemistry and physics requirements and was soon released. I went to work for the Central Medical Committee but the CMC did not satisfy my patriotic urge and I decided to follow my older sister's steps and go into nurses training. That didn't last and soon I joined the ATS, the women's branch of the Army.

We were sent to the Isle of Man to train as special wireless operators. We soon became operational. Only now, after I have seen the program "Enigma" do I know what we were doing as we sat at our radio sets, eight hours on, eight hours off, and a day off after every four shifts, for three years.

Victory came in 1945. We celebrated when my brother returned from POW camp.

I was accepted for one of the new library schools in 1947. I was interested in working in a medical library. I did not have a university degree but I got the chance to go in on the ground floor of the Royal Society of Medicine.

I immigrated to New Zealand in 1952. I knew I had to start a new life after losing my heart to a man I could not marry. Both my eldest sister and youngest brother and their spouses had already immigrated and they helped me with housing and jobs. In just one year I was librarian of the New Zealand Department of Health. I was responsible for library collections in the district offices and psychiatric hospitals throughout New Zealand.

At the end of 1954, I received a letter from the Librarian of the University of Western Ontario, in Canada, offering me a job. A colleague, who was the Librarian at the Royal Society of Medicine, had recommended me. There were no vacancies in the medical school library but if I would start in the general library, I could transfer when a vacancy occurred. I accepted the offer and arrived by boat in Vancouver, British Colombia, on January 3, 1 955. I was transferred to the medical school library and perhaps I would still be there if I had not had a run-in with the big boss. I began looking for another job. I thought I would take a look at the United States. In 1958, I accepted a cataloging job in the library of Antioch College, Yellow Springs, Ohio.

Within a year, after a somewhat turbulent courtship, I married a widower with two sons, Don, sixteen, and Fred, eleven. I am glad that I did not know what was in store for me. I had been in America for little more than a year, I knew little about American boys and schools and less about washing machines and dishwashers. I could not cook and was not used to shopping for four. In a way, life became easier when I found I was pregnant and the next year, I presented the family with a baby girl whom we named Hilary. When she was nine months old I looked at my incomplete degree work and found I could finish it with correspondence courses, summer school and electives at Antioch.

At thirty-nine years old I was quite happy. I was blessed with a beautiful family, and had a delightful German neighbor with young children who gladly took Hilary when I was studying and coached me for my German course.

In the summer of 1962, I returned to summer school. I passed my courses and received my Bachelor's of Art degree in October. After receiving my degree, I contracted for a six months job at Antioch. When my contract was up I looked around for another part-time library job and found one at Wilberforce University. Wilberforce had been the first black college operated by blacks. It was a wonderful time to be there, which was during the Civil Rights activity.

In 1973, Howard took an early retirement and in September of that year both my mother and eldest sister died and Howard was not well. He was admitted to the hospital for exploratory surgery and died suddenly. My second sister had died the year before. Life was lonely.

At fifty-one, I decided that it was the time to be my own woman. I wanted to go back to school. I wanted to be a social worker and applied to Wright State University social work department in the following fall and found I could use most of my Canadian degree credits toward another Bachelor's degree. I also started working as a student volunteer in the social services department of a hospital and was soon on a cardiac rehabilitation team. It took two years to complete the required classes and I ended with an internship at the local mental health department. I was encouraged to go on to graduate school and entered the University of Louisville, Kentucky, and graduated in 1977.

My children were scattered. Hilary was in San Jose, California, Don in British Columbia, and Fred was in Bellingham, Washington. I decided to move to Bellingham. I traveled to the United Kingdom and New Zealand and made a disastrous marriage, which ended in divorce. In 1982, I moved to Lummi Island and learned to live alone. I liked it. I enjoyed the company of my sheltie and my cat, creatures that have taught me a lot about living.

In 1990, things changed again rapidly. I visited my friend Kate in Boise, Idaho, and I met her uncle, Al Neece. He persuaded me to extend a weekend visit into a week. In no time we were a couple. But this time it has worked.

I have found niches that have kept my life structured, such as Learning Lab, Log Cabin, doing *tai chi* and the Parent Educator Organization. I believe that everything I have done has served a purpose.

My spiritual path has been a winding one. Raised very traditionally, I have done a lot of exploring and questioning in my life and am still not sure what I believe. As a child I thought God was a mix of King George and Santa Claus. Sometimes I claim I am agnostic and continue to ponder, although I am certain that God is beyond my comprehension.

In order to keep going I think we need a dream that we can be in command of. I view the future with levity and some apprehension. As Karen, my poet friend, says, "Trust life." Everything can be quite simple if we let it. Fear not.

It is of immense importance
that we laugh at ourselves.

— Katharine Mansfield

Susie Stoval

"Grannie's Favorite Rooster"

Some of my earliest and fondest memories are of my grandfather and the wonderful times that we spent together. Grandpa passed away in 1970 but I think about him almost every day.

Grandpa always has been and always will be my special hero. I am convinced that Grandpa was the only person who ever truly understood me. He proved that many times through the years, but never more than in the case of Grannie's favorite old rooster.

The incident happened when I was four years old. Of all of the fowls my grandmother owned, her favorite was a scrawny old Dommenicker rooster that she called Brady. Brady had one eye. He had lost the other in a fight when he was a young cock, years before I was born. He walked funny because both legs had been broken at least once.

One time when Brady was flogging me, Grandpa heard my screaming and came to my rescue. He only meant to kick Brady away from me but he kicked much harder than he realized.

I begged for Grandpa to kill old Brady for hurting me but he said that he couldn't because Grandma would have his hide if he did. He agreed with me that Brady was the meanest old cuss of a rooster that ever lived and that something terrible would happen to him if he ever hurt me again. Grandpa promised that Brady would no longer harm me. He told me that this incident would be our secret because it would only distress Grandma if she knew what had happened. We agreed to tell Grandma that we had found Brady in the horse corral and that one of the horses had most likely stepped on him.

Grandpa scooped Brady up and we took him to the house where Grandma put a splint on his leg and put him in a special pen close to the house so that he could recover while Grandma kept her eye on him.

A few weeks later, Brady was completely recovered and again the terror of territory. As usual, I kept close to Grandpa while he worked about the place. I remember one day when he was working on a saddle in the tack room. I was helping him when Brady came strutting (hobbling) by. As always, he seemed to be giving me the evil eye. My grandpa was busy and wasn't paying attention to my childish prattle. I told him that I was going to kill that rooster before he got to me. Grandpa grunted and told me to go ahead. His head was down and I could see he was busy but I thought that he had given me his blessing to kill old Brady.

I looked for a weapon. I picked up a hatchet from a workbench and marched to do battle with Brady. Brady ruffled his feathers and with a squawk, he tried to bounce into the air. When he couldn't get off the ground, he waddled forth to meet me halfway. He took his best shot, but before he could turn and launch another attack, I took mine. I swung the hatchet and it connected. Old Brady fell to his side, kicked a few times, and then he lay still. I felt queasy but proud as I marched back to Grandpa and told him what had happened. Grandpa glanced up from his work and caught sight of the hatchet with blood and feathers sticking to it and said, "Oh Lord, Nee-Pee, what the hell have you done to your grandmother's old rooster?"

It was then that I decided that I had made a mistake. After all, old Brady was Grandma's favorite. And he must have been very special to her or he would have been in the dumpling pot years ago. I began to cry.

Grandpa picked me up, took the bloody hatchet out of my hand, and dried my tears with his handkerchief. "Now, Nee-Pee, we'll give Brady a nice quiet funeral and we won't say anything about this to your grandma. If she begins to worry we will suggest that a coyote or fox probably got Brady.

Grandpa got a shovel and we buried old Brady. I said a prayer over the old cock for Grandma's sake.

To our surprise, Grandma didn't seem to question Brady's whereabouts. She reassured me that Brady was probably in rooster heaven. For weeks I made up remarkable stories about where I thought Brady was or what might have happened to him. Grandma would always reassure me that Brady was okay, dead or alive.

It was many years later that I learned from one of her sisters that on the fateful day of Brady's death, Grandma had been in the calving pasture helping a young heifer deliver her first calf. She had witnessed the whole killing scene but was too far away and too busy to help me. She told my aunt that she never worried about the incident because she knew that Grandpa would take care of his "Nee-Pee."

Susie Stoval wrote this story for a creative writing class at the Center for the Blind and Visually Impaired.

The necessity for patience had aged her magically,
she was content in her age.

— Joyce Carol Oates

Ann Vycital

Memories

A question nags at the recess of my mind
Where is he? Is he alive?
And does he remember?
Though life left us down separate pathways,
When we were young,
Once we deeply cared
Before a war that changed so many lives
We cared. With naiveté
We dreamed sweet dreams
But distance, and time and the river of life
Flowed gently into different streams.
With memories our only tie,
I wonder where currents have taken him,
If his passage was smooth
And
If he ever remembers.

— Ann Vycital

As I slipped my eight-year old body between the feather bed and heavy quilts, my cold feet reached for the poor-man's makeshift heating pad, a Mason jar full of hot water and I stopped shivering. Then I remembered Mother's parting remark. "Ann," she said, her shoulders slumping with fatigue, "be sure and mop up the water you spilled before you go to bed." I procrastinated and wondered why I should bother. It would evaporate by morning anyway, I thought. Entering the kitchen the next morning, I slipped and fell on the puddle, now frozen to hard ice.

"You will be the cause of most everything that happens to you in life," Mother admonished, "It will be easier if you learn responsibility."

That was one of many lessons I learned from my wonderful, unselfish and supportive parents who struggled to raise seven children in a broken-down farmhouse that was always in need of Dad's handy hands.

Though I grew up in poverty, I grew up in a loving and fun family environment. I learned to read by a kerosene lamp and always wore hand-me-downs, but life was full of excitement. I had horses to ride, haystacks to slide down and Mother's hot cinnamon rolls to eat upon returning from school.

I was also taught that an education was important. "Go to Chicago," Mother would say, "get an education and get out of the farm mud." And I did.

Choices for women were limited to secretaries, schoolteachers or nurses. I earned my Registered Nurses Degree during World War II. My greatest challenge was to endure the nine– to twelve-hour-a-day hospital working shifts while continuing my education. Most women worked in the factories for war supplies so few aides were in the hospital. My saddest experience of neglect came while I was a night nurse on duty in the men's ward at Cook County Hospital. With seventy patients in large charity wards and only one aide, we admitted the wounded (usually stab wounds from the Chicago slums), gave medications and removed the dead. We did it all.

The war ended and a few months later, I graduated. I took a post-grad course at an Illinois research hospital where I met an impoverished intern. The first time I saw his name in print I thought, Poor man, imagine having to go through life with a name like that. Soon after we met, I joined him in the Vycital name.

After marriage we both worked hard to finance Dick's surgical residency. Soon after I delivered our second child, the Korean War broke out and Dick was called back into the Air Force. We moved to France.

In 1952, at three o'clock in the morning on the high seas between France and New York, on our way back to the United States, Dick awakened me with a whisper, "I want to move out west," he said. "I don't want stay in Chicago."

I was elated. I too was ready for new territory.

We went to Chicago and packed our belongings in a truck, said our good-byes to family and friends and headed west. We settled in Boise, Idaho, with a population of 42,000. I remember gazing at the mountains, thinking that we were home, this was the place where we would raise our children, meet new friends, live our lives, and die.

The next several years passed quickly with usual school PTA meetings, girl and Boy Scout meetings, children's church choir practice and pounding nails into our old cabin in McCall. We raised our two children, both of whom earned two college degrees and were thirty years old when they married.

As soon as the nest was empty, Dick began traveling to various countries doing volunteer medical work. I went with him on some of the trips. We were in Nome, Alaska, American Samoa, India, and at one time Dick was the only doctor on the tiny island of Barbuda.

Everywhere we traveled, I was impressed with the difficulties faced by women. In Nome, in addition to the bitter cold, water for household use was rationed and delivered in tank trucks. In Samoa, I was touched by the apparent gentleness of the people, only to learn of the violence in their tribal culture and the dictatorial and chauvinistic power of the tribal chief.

Other Americans told us, "Never sleep on your back with your mouth open." Nine-inch lizards hunted cockroaches on walls and ceilings and sometimes they would release a part of the captured bug or even their own droppings.

In Barbuda, men and women both suffered high blood pressure and kidney disease from the drinking water that contained large amounts of sodium. Housekeeping had its challenges. I had to sift the huge weevils from the flour when baking. And twice a week we would pour a cup of Clorox into our water supply to remove the bacteria. But the spiders and frogs didn't seem to mind.

In India, I lectured on breast cancer detection, only to find the incidence of breast cancer is extremely low. But I always had a large audience, thanks to their curiosity and unfailing courtesy.

While in the country, I learned of the prevalence of burning brides to death. At times, it was suicide due to harsh treatment but more often it was due to an unhappy husband or mother-in-law over a dowry disagreement. I was also informed of the women being circumcised (often without anesthetic). This barbaric practice was inflicted upon the woman so that she could not enjoy sex and infidelity would be less likely. The law gave women little or no protection and they often died from infection after weeks of agonizing pain. A woman is now ruler of the country so progress is being made but as with most changes it takes time and patience.

Dick died several years ago. He is buried at Dry Creek Cemetery. I am grateful for his love and his dedication to family and medicine. He taught me that excessive wealth has nothing to do with happiness. But that love holds the key to all things, especially to happiness.

We are blessed to live in America. And even though injustice against women at times continues, nowhere else are we so fortunate and free. Marriages are not arranged. We can marry for love, remain single, choose from a myriad of professions and fight for our rights in court. In the decades of women's liberation, I have enjoyed the uniqueness of being a woman. Most men are conditioned to protect their mate. Perhaps because I am from the older generation, I have enjoyed men treating me as a lady instead of as an equal. I think that the men who are courteous and protective have not lost but instead, have gained strength and masculinity. I do not feel less powerful or less capable when a door is opened for me and I enjoy the warm caress of a coat being placed on my shoulder. I worry that women of today, in gaining so much, may lose too much. I enjoy and admire women enormously but I love men, too, and savor their company. As I learned in France, "Viva le difference."

It occurred to me when I was thirteen
and wearing white gloves and Mary Janes
and going to dancing school, that no one should
have to dance backward all their lives.

— Jill Ruckelshaus

Alice Dieter

"Follow your bliss."

Careers begin someplace only because life is a series of tangles, and untangling the web of circumstance requires too much effort. I could credit my career's beginning to the rain, or maybe to the telephone sales call. Or I might reluctantly admit to a certain intellectual arrogance to explain what happened.

It was rainy that Sunday morning in June 1963. As we left St. Michael's Cathedral, Rick Raphael was also coming down the front steps. Rick was a friend, an intense and effective reporter for the local CBS radio-television channel, KBOI Channel 2. The station had recently purchased *The Idaho Observer,* a weekly shopping guide being transformed into a newspaper. I had just subscribed to *The Observer,* biting on a telephone sales pitch describing the paper as appealing to "the intelligent segment of the community." That segment must include me, of course.

What I didn't know was that conventional wisdom at that time dictated a "women's page" as a necessity to build newspaper subscriber lists. To create such a page for *The Observer* the editor bought a syndicated feature, "Heloise's Household Hints". Heloise provided an unequalled compendium of ways women could clean, garnish, and renew everything but the intellect. I was betrayed.

Rick was listed as the science editor of *The Idaho Observer,* and he was near at hand that morning, so I expressed my outrage to him. He was amused and teasing. "Yeah? Well the choir sang flat today, but I don't want to go to choir rehearsals so I'm not complaining."

We went our separate ways. The rain continued. No gardening for me on that afternoon. The kids played next door. The house was quiet and Rick's banter rankled. My portable typewriter, unused since college days, came down from the top shelf in the storage closet and was dusted off. Resentment churned, but so did imagination. Even a mere ex-high school paper editor could do better than Heloise.

I spent the afternoon building a list of suggested feature stories that would appeal to the "intelligent female reader," me. The more I built the list the more fascinating the possibilities seemed.

By Wednesday, I had an interview appointment with my tennis instructor after our Boise City Recreation Ladies Day class. Barbara Chandler was an ideal subject. She came to Boise ranked tenth nationally in women's professional tennis, and her presence launched a tennis renaissance in the community. She was a great interview.

I marched up the stairs at the KBOI Building and into the editor's office with list, interview and photograph in hand. I told an astonished and defenseless man (Harry Bodine, later editor at the *Portland Oregonian)* what I thought of "Heloise" and how I thought he ought to run his newspaper if he wanted to interest ME. Which I assumed he did. I was brash, arrogant, naïve and had no intention of looking for a job.

He printed the interview. I saw my byline in print. I was hooked.

I kept on favoring Harry with my efforts and a month or so later he paid me $3 for a piece. I was thirty-five years old and had never been paid to do what I liked to do, write. All the news releases and PR work I had previously devoted to the League of Women Voters and other volunteer organizations suddenly looked like internship for entry into the real world of paid, professional journalism. That first check was only $3. It made no difference to the family budget. But to me it meant recognition, adulthood, identity and acceptance in the world where, like it or not, money was the perceived measure of value.

I was intensely interested in politics, social issues and how people thought and acted. I followed those interests. I sought recognition and loved being a big frog in a very small puddle. As feminist consciousness evolved, I wanted to change the social terms that had rendered me so naïve and unimportant in the larger world. And I love the craft of writing.

I found wonderful mentors along the way, both men and women. I had encouragement and help in the home. I didn't head to an office before the youngest of our three children was in kindergarten. And I was very lucky.

Eventually, the occasional freelance work with *The Idaho Observer,* later known as *The Intermountain Observer,* evolved into an office job as assistant editor. The editor who replaced Bodine was a brilliant newspaperman, Sam Day. He was challenging, demanding and enamored of taking issues to the barricades. In the sixties and early seventies, he drew around him controversy and a small but avid readership. He gave me the chance to be in the midst of issues swirling around poverty, social justice and the Vietnam War.

Sam also had the remarkable ability to teach without seeming to do so. He saw instantly how small events fit the pattern of larger societal issues. He wrote, and still writes, extremely well and his editing was unrelenting. The newspaper was witty, challenging and uncompromising in addressing political and social problems. It won national recognition.

We wrote about education in the public schools and Idaho's institutions of higher education. I wrote the decade-long story as Boise Junior College fought its way into state college status and grew to a university. Our publisher put us into the middle of an unsuccessful effort to develop a medical school in Boise. We covered the first efforts for urban renewal in the city. We exposed acts of racial discrimination. We battled for the rights of welfare women. I even covered a prison riot at the old prison on Warm Springs Avenue when Sam was out of town and I saw the glow of fire in the old cellblocks from my home on the hills above. (Prison reform was one of Sam's concerns.)

Banishing "Heloise," I developed a page that covered drama, music and art with serious news treatment and critical comment. It was a page for women and men. We spread our readership net statewide. We had travel and phone budgets underwritten by the radio/television operation to help make this possible.

We wrote for all three media (newspaper, radio and television) because of the co-ownership. And with the happenstance of getting pictures of a fatal plane crash on Galena Summit above Sun Valley, I became the first woman on Idaho television to go on camera as a regular reporter. (The photo was of Idaho Congresswoman Louise Shadduck carrying a dead infant from the crash site, her face stricken with grief and shock. It won an award in photography from the Idaho Press Club that year.)

That breakthrough led to regular television reporting assignments. My arrogance helped when I told KBOI's news director, Dick Eardley (later the mayor of Boise), that he was "wasting" my talents using me to file film halftime, something a high school intern could do. Dick agreed, I suspect, reluctantly. He didn't think women's voices sounded "authoritative" enough to be on the news. But social change was coming and the turmoil of the sixties was bringing women and ethnically different faces to the TV screen hitherto the sole domain of white males.

In 1974, media change hit television in less congenial ways. Newscasts began to drift toward the entertainment emphasis that distorts the profession now (in the year 2000). Cameras and film developing and editing techniques improved and dramatic pictures began to take precedence and airtime from hard news and talking heads. Short clips of information pushed longer, explanatory information aside. Youth, glamour and "happy talk" style was displacing the direct, sometimes acerbic delivery that newspapermen had brought to the news media. And I was in my mid-forties.

The Observer meanwhile had separated from KBOI when Sam's activism, and finally his civil disobedience, made the paper too hot for the corporate ownership to continue to tolerate. The loyal readership bought "stock" in the paper, which continued on its own for a couple of years. Then Sam retired the masthead with honor and sold the legal identity with its lucrative legal advertising. I continued with the station but I knew my time in the new era was also on the wane. And it wasn't as much fun without Sam who eventually left Boise to edit the prestigious *Bulletin of the Atomic Scientists* in Chicago.

One day at my desk I received a call from an unfamiliar voice. Mike Silva, newly hired at Boise Cascade Corporation to write and edit a quarterly company magazine, called to ask if I were interested in changing jobs and would I meet for lunch. I said that I didn't know about the job but I would meet him.

For better and for worse I took the job as his assistant. Writing for a corporation is a different kettle of fish than writing for a freewheeling social advocacy newspaper. In a little over ten years, my pay scale increased by magnitudes of thousands. There was (for a time) considerable travel and I learned to handle airlines and hotels and taxies and rental cars.

I found the corporation was also a community. It had to be explored for contacts and confidences, mined for ideas and explained to its many audiences. I wrote feature stories, news briefs, speeches and benefit insurance information. I learned about office politics, inner corporate conflicts, power plays and treachery. I learned the art of the office memo. I learned to tailor my craft and temper my individuality. It paid well, but it was never as much fun as the newspaper days.

What was fun was writing a freelance weekly column for the editorial page of *The Idaho Statesman.* The invitation to do so came from the editorial page editor Jim Boyd, who later moved on to the editorial desk of *The Minneapolis Tribune.* Jim said he wanted a "feminist perspective," and the column was my unfettered outlet every Wednesday for eight years until a successor to Jim dropped me. My replacement was the former governor of the state, Robert Smylie.

Being dropped infuriated me for all of forty-five seconds. Then a flood of relief replaced fury and hurt; for the first time in more than twenty years, I had no deadline to meet. I had negotiated an early retirement from Boise Cascade two years earlier.

And now, for over fifteen years I have been retired, a misnomer perhaps. All of the preceding history seems a mere preparation for the privilege of being in the now, the present. This time, the return to volunteer status is an achievement rather than a negation. And I find myself following the same impulses and interests with which my story began. I have less physical energy but a hell of a lot more understanding.

I am intensely curious about people and issues, angered by injustice, motivated by a belief that my life matters in the universal scheme. I refuse to be bored. I love to write. I have a multitude of experiences to draw on. I relish speaking, teaching and being part of what I choose to care about. I revel in the love, companionship and support of the man I linked my life with fifty-four years ago. I believe that Joseph Campbell had it right when he said, "Follow your bliss."

Eileen Keith

"You can touch many lives with calls and letters and never leave home."

I was born on March 15, 1925. I grew up in the Lakeview community, south of Lake Lowell, Idaho. There was my father, Eph, mother Mary and two brothers, Laurel and Jesse. Dad farmed property belonging to Anna Young. She was the sister of C.C. Anderson who founded The Golden Rule stores, which later became the Bon Marche. Anna was a wonderful lady.

Dad had dairy cows, chickens, and pigs. We had fruit trees and each year grew a beautiful garden. Our house was small with two bedrooms, a sleeping porch, a living room and a kitchen. We used oil lamps for light until the Coleman Lanterns came along. In the living room we had an old fashion wood/coal stove, which we used for heat. In the evening after chores, we would gather around the stove and play cards and tell stories.

We attended Lakeview School. It consisted of two large rooms with four grades on each side and one teacher in one room. I remember every May 1 when the town of Nampa would get together at the school and gather around the flagpole for the May Day festivities.

My brother Jesse used to drive us to school in Mom and Dad's Whippet (a type of automobile). One day I loaded all of my friends in the car for a ride. I put the car in reverse and began to roll down the hill. The car stopped when it got stuck in a barrow pit. I went home that day in big trouble.

We created our own fun as children. We played kick the can, cops and robbers, and tag. After the evening fun, I would come indoors to see Mom and Dad sitting in front of the radio listening to Amos and Andy, Burns and Allen or the Grand Old Opry.

My sister Angela was born in 1933. Four years after Angela's birth, my mother died. My dad, brothers and I had to learn to cook, clean and take care of a small child. I had to cook for the hay crew. With the school's permission I took Angela to school with me.

During my sophomore year, we moved to Marsing. Dad farmed for Lena Volkmer. Lena is a special lady whom I regarded as my other mom. I attended Marsing High School. It was a small school blessed with dedicated teachers. We were all very close. A popular hangout was the soda fountain at Tailors Drug Store. We swam at Givens Hot Springs and went to dances every weekend.

My father passed away in February 1943. My brother Laurel lost his arm in a tractor accident the next month. It was a difficult year. My brother Jesse and his wife Ernie came to help run the farm. Ernie brought her brother Bill to help on the farm. One morning when I went out to the barn, Bill was milking a cow. It was love at first sight.

Bill and I were married on September 4, 1943. One month later, Bill left for Marine Boot Camp. And in February 1944, he was shipped overseas. I made my home with Bill's family in Boise and worked at the Splendid Bakery for a few months until I went to work for the Office of

Price Administration. Meat, sugar, shoes, gas and tires were rationed during the war. Price Administration approved and issued the books of stamps and permits to the public so the office was not always popular.

Bill and I kept in touch by writing letters during the two years he was away. He fought in Okinawa and Peleliu. After the surrender, he was stationed in China for a short while.

Bill returned from the war on February 27, 1946, and took a job as an apprentice electrician for Alloway Electric. When Sears opened their new store, I went to work in the customer service. We built a home where we raised our three boys, Doug, Del and Dennis, and our daughter, Debra. Money was tight but we managed a drive in movie once a week.

In 1953, Bill went to work for his brother who owned Enterprise Electric. He was offered the business in 1964. We purchased Enterprise and worked together. We were able to run the business and be home with the children. We were involved with their sports, music, scouts and school activities.

Life was splendid until October 31, 1973, when Bill suffered a devastating heart attack at the age of forty-nine. He had open-heart surgery and recuperated very well. Our son Doug joined us at Enterprise. We were able to take care of Bill and the business from the home. Since that first attack Bill has had his fill of surgeries and hospital stays but he is a fighter and continues to thrive.

I retired from Enterprise in 1983 when Doug and his wife Jean took over the business. In 1984, Bill and I built a cabin in Centerville, Idaho, where we have spent most of our retirement.

I am currently serving on the board of the Sacred Heart School Foundation. It has been challenging yet rewarding.

Our sons Doug and Delbert continue to operate Enterprise Electric. Dennis works for Hewlett Packard and our daughter Debra and her husband Mike live in Huntsville, Alabama. Debra was diagnosed with Multiple Sclerosis in 1991. She is doing well. She is a fighter like her father.

Through the years, I have tried to pass on to others what I have learned myself, which is to be kind and to share my knowledge with those around me. As I get older, my desire to communicate with those around me becomes more intense. And even though it has been difficult to reach out in person, I have found that I can touch many lives with calls and letters and never leave home.

Novella Hart

"What a different world it is now. How often we hear that said, and how fantastically true it is."

When I was three, I asked my mother, "How did we meet Grandma?' I don't know what her answer was but I do know I have always been intrigued by the idea of family connections. Who came from where, and when? My paternal grandmother died during the great flu epidemic after World War I and my grandfather soon after, so most of my musings had to do with my female lineage on my mother's side, my mother, grandmother and great-grandmother.

I feel a strong connection with those three women who came before me. What kind of life did they have? What games did they play as children? What did they look like? And how different were their lives from mine?

My great-grandmother, Susanna Stucki, was born in Switzerland in 1842. I have been to the village where she was born in the Simmenthal Valley of the Bernese Alps and marveled at the beauty of its green valleys and great white peaks. But her life must have been difficult, with long cold winters and summers filled with preparation for the next winter.

In her early teens, Susanna went to work in the home of Gottleib Scheiben, my great- grandfather, the Burgomeister of Oberwil. She was a spinster in her early thirties when Gottleib's wife died in childbirth leaving the baby and several other children motherless. It would seem to have been for practical reasons that Gottleib took Susanna for his wife but the marriage thrived long enough for her to bear him six more children, beginning with my grandmother, Karolina, when Susanna was thirty-three.

Several years later we visited the little village of Oberwil. I saw the house where my grandmother was born. But as the first and oldest child in the second half of what would become a family of thirteen children, her responsibility for keeping them each fed and clothed must have been a challenge for a young girl. I was not surprised when I learned that Grandmother went to New York in the company of an uncle when she was fifteen and never returned to Switzerland or her family again.

When she arrived at Ellis Island, she spoke German, Swiss and French, but no English. Later, I found her broken English charming but I imagine how difficult her first years in that enormous city must have been. She was employed as an upstairs maid for a wealthy family and, from what I knew of my grandmother, I am certain that she was a good employee. She was neat and meticulous. I rarely saw her without an apron, a dust cloth, broom or cooking spoon in her hand. There are undocumented rumors in the family that she became pregnant by the eldest son of the couple she worked for. She went West after the birth of the child, alone.

There is uncertainty as to how Carrie (the name she chose for her life in the new country) found herself living in the Canadian mid-west. That is where she met my grandfather, Christopher Coates. They had a hard life living on a farm homestead. My grandfather worked for the railroad. My grandmother kept busy with indoor and outdoor chores. She made good use of the skills remembered from the old country, making butter and cheese, working in the fields and cooking for the many harvesters.

My mother Ruth was the third of six children born to Carrie and Chris. In some ways her life as a young girl was not different from her grandmother, Susanna Stucki. But instead of a farm on the steep hillside of a Swiss valley, the wide flat plains of the Canadian prairies were home to her.

My mother's life encompassed incredible changes from that of Carrie and Susanna. Before she died at the age of eighty-six, she had seen the world progress in every facet of living.

Mother was seventeen in 1917 when she and my father Chester Cochran were married. My father told me that the most beautiful thing he ever saw was his first glimpse of my mother flying across a field, bareback on a horse, with her mass of dark, curly hair flying out behind her. She had a wonderful sense of humor and the calm ability to accept whatever life brought. This must have helped her to see through the dark years of World War I. Their eldest son was born when my father was in France during the war. He died before my father ever saw him.

I was born when mother was twenty-five, in 1925. I grew up in the world of the Great Depression. We lived for the first eight years of my life in a house with electricity (which was only a bulb on a wire that hung in each room) but without running hot water or indoor plumbing, without a radio, and without a school bus to take us to school. We walked three-and-a-half miles to school until the sixth grade. We lived in a small logging town in the Puget Sound area of Washington. Our neighbors were

Scandinavian so I grew up among Olsens, Rasmussens, Johnsons and Jensens.

The Depression came. I knew we were strapped for money but I never felt poor or any different from everyone else we knew. The only people I thought of as wealthy were the Rasmussens, the family of a man who was a foreman in the paper mill. They lived in the big yellow house on the hill. I remember someone telling me that his salary was $50 a week. His wife Rhetta, who everyone called Rappy, was a gregarious, happy-go-lucky woman who weighed an awesome three hundred pounds. She was the best cook in the neighborhood. It was Rappy who taught me to cook. She was the unofficial caterer of many events and I loved to help her prepare for wedding receptions, church dinners or lodge suppers.

What a different world it is now. How often we hear that said, and how fantastically true it is. I would love to go back to see Susanna going about her chores or marrying Gottleib in the little church with the witches'-cap steeple, or holding her little Karolina for baptism in that same little church in the meadow. I have stood on the altar of the church imagining Karolina in her mother's arms. I have imagined the long journey for her to America and her marriage to Christopher.

As my daughters, granddaughters, and great-granddaughters become my age what a treasure they will have in the records I have kept.

There are so many memories yet to be played out and so many more stories to be told. The beauty of heritage is that it is everlasting in the hearts of those who choose to remember and who choose to hold on.

Luann Crump

"...if I had known that everything works out, I would have relaxed and enjoyed the present more."

I was born on October 6, 1932, in Minneapolis, Minnesota. My brother James was four and a half at the time. My father worked for the Minneapolis Parks Department and managed the local golf course. Even though I lived on a golf course, I didn't golf. In contrast, my brother was very athletic and was on the golf team. As a teenager, I had asthma and felt that I missed out on a lot of things my friends did. I was worried about getting sick.

I lived with my parents while I went to the University of Minnesota where I worked toward a BA in Sociology. During college, I worked at related jobs — the YWCA in New York, and with migrant children in Oregon. Following graduation, I moved to Fresno, California, where I worked for the Girl Scouts, organizing troops among the migrant workers.

It was in Fresno that I met William Crump at a singles church group. We were married when I was 27. William was a geographer but was working as an insurance salesman. Our first two children, William III and Jeffrey, were born in Fresno. My husband went back to school to become a teacher and then taught Social Studies at the junior high school level. Later we moved to Columbus, Ohio, where he earned a Master's and Ph.D. in Geography and Social Studies Education. During this time, I worked as a program director for the Girl Scout Council; our daughter, Anna, was born as well. Following my husband's graduation, we moved to Pocatello, Idaho, where he taught Social Studies Education at Idaho State University. I worked for the school system in the Head Start program.

When we both were 41, my husband died from a melanoma that had invaded his lymph system. The children were nine, seven, and two. Being single following the death of my husband was very hard, especially the loneliness. We had a very loving relationship and I have wonderful memories of this.

I continued working for the Head Start program and completed a Master's in Adult Education at Idaho State University. In 1977, I moved to Boise as director of the Girl Scouts, where I soon learned that girl programs were discounted next to boys. Girl Scouts had equal or more challenges, innovative programs and learning opportunities as Boy Scouts. But at the time, the perception was that girl programs were just busy work. However, our mission was accomplished and we gave many women leadership opportunities.

I retired from the Girls Scouts in 1995. Since retirement, I have traveled and have taken classes at BSU, especially watercolor classes. I have gone to Italy and Switzerland with the Watercolor Society and, in 2000, I will go to Provence, France, with this group. I love to travel. My grandparents came over from Sweden and I have been to Europe many times. My husband and I traveled across Canada by train for our honeymoon. We went to Iceland and England for our tenth wedding anniversary. My son Jeffrey married a woman from the Czech Republic. I went to the wedding, which was held in a small church in Moravia where the bride's grandmother was buried. My daughter-in-law is an Art Historian and was the curator of the local castle. They now live in New York City. My daughter Ann is a chemist and works for Kodak in Medford, Oregon. My other son, Dr. Bill Crump III, is a family practice physician at St. Luke's Medical Center in Meridian.

My community activities include the Episcopal Church on the local, state and national levels, Girl Scouts, Head Start, the American Association of University Women, watercolor and garden clubs. I am now writing family stories for my children and grandchildren and have taken courses in writing at BSU. I have chronic lymphatic leukemia for which I received chemotherapy in 1999. My doctor says I am doing much better than he expected.

I didn't have a lot of confidence during my early life but prayer helped me get through. I have learned how life fits together and if I had known everything works out I would have relaxed and enjoyed the present more. My advice to others is to have a positive attitude, see that glass as half full, not half empty, to expect changes in life and see them as opportunities.

Laughter can be more satisfying than honor;
more precious than money;
more heart cleansing than prayer.

— Harriet Rochlin

The Dotage Party

"When I am an old woman I shall . . ."

Three good friends living in Boise, Idaho, celebrated their sixtieth birthdays within the same two months. They invited their many women friends to a Saturday afternoon tea party. Wearing old-fashioned hats, the hostesses served tea, champagne, and presented a resplendent table full of petits fours, chocolate creams, lemon bars, scones, and other irresistible delights.

The program began with one of the guests reciting from memory and with excellent interpretation, Jenny Joseph's poem. "When I am an old woman I shall wear purple." After this the company broke into groups of ten. The hostesses gave everyone a piece of paper pre-printed with the words at the top. "When I am an old woman I shall . . ." Each person created the next line of her own version of the poem and passed the paper to her neighbor on the left. The next person wrote a second line on the paper and so on until it rounded the circle and came back to the author of the first line, who then wrote the last line to complete the poem. The poets were invited to read their poems aloud, which they did.

When I am an old woman I shall . . .

Take a train from east to west and eat a lot of toast
Drink beer and dance
But don't you think I go too far?
I might dance on a table in a bar
And drive a convertible car
I will break all the mirrors
Or perhaps go to Hollywood for a full body liposuction
Dye my hair red and the take the train back.

When I am an old woman I shall . . .

Live dangerously and not worry how I look
Only concerns will be which book to read next
Or should it be a poem or a lovely text
Or the latest movie, full of passion
Or the next concert, played on the village green
Or a weekend retreat with Buddhist monks
Or fly down the mountain on my skies.

When I am an old woman I shall . . .

Have nothing but fun
But alas, I will be the only one.
But not for long, I will answer ads in the romantic press
Charming, passionate, originality and neatness
Requesting a six-foot handsome senior, not on Viagra
Find joy with a young poet.
Give gratitude for estrogen vaginal cream
Dance all night and sleep all day
Except when there is something more interesting to do
Drive to the mountains in a fast car
Or neck on the mountain with a fast man.

Inez G. Dotson

"We had an old car, but not enough money to buy gas."

In 1917, I was born in Cambridge, Idaho, and I have lived here my entire life. My father and grandfather moved from Wisconsin to homestead in 1890. I have a sister who is six years older than me and she has always been an inspiration to me.

When I married, I thought it would be just what I wanted. My husband and I lived out of town on the ranch. We raised chickens and milked cows, selling the eggs for nine cents a dozen, and the cream for three or four dollars a week. Having four children, three daughters and a son, I enjoyed the busy life that raising a family brings. When they were small, I sewed snowsuits and coats out of old coats and material. I've always been a housewife and homemaker, there every day when the children returned from school.

There were bad times during the Depression years and we didn't have much to live on. We had an old car, but not enough money to buy gas. During World War II, my husband's name was called for the draft. We were worried but he wasn't called to go. My sister's only son was in the Korean War at Pork Chop Hill, where many young soldiers died beside him. We are blessed that he came home. Ten years ago, he had a successful heart transplant.

When we were young, we attended all of the dances, where we would really have a great time. I never took part in many community activities, only when the kids were in something. I belong to the PTA, the Mission, and First Baptist Church of Cambridge, where I attend Bible study.

My biggest challenge was always trying to keep peace in the family and keeping my husband from getting upset with the family. I would say this has been the hardest because I didn't want anyone to be angry with anyone. I think the turning point was when the children married and had homes of their own and my husband and I were alone at home.

I think everyone has regrets and think they could have done more thoughtful things for their loved ones. It means a lot to me to still live where I was born. I feel I am a very good wife and mother and that our children have good memories of me. I worked hard at everything I did and tried to be everything I should. I have really learned a lot and realize that I could have done many things differently. Thinking back, I would not marry so young and I would have done more in my younger years.

We are a close family and enjoy many activities together, including picnicking and camping and vacations. We have gone on several trips with our son and his wife in a camper. Just up in Canada and Northern California.

At my age, I want to be more kind and thoughtful of everyone and do good deeds for them. I like needlework and do a lot of crocheting and embroidering. I like to read a lot and learn as much as I can. Being kind and thoughtful of everyone and taking care to set a good example is important to me.

Margaret Fuller

"I earn money for what I love to do . . . hike."

Going to the mountains has been one of my favorite things since I can remember. It became important because as a child I spent my father's vacations at my grandfather's mountain cabin. My grandfather, one of the original professors at Stanford law school, built the kitchen of the cabin in 1912. The board and batten cabin looked down a hundred feet onto a blue wedge of Fallen Leaf Lake.

My father was a CPA and although my mother had a Masters in Economics, she spent my growing years as a homemaker, raising me, my brother Tom, who is three years younger than me, and my sister Dodie, six years younger. (My father loved to hike, so that is what we usually did during his vacations.)

At first I did not like hiking because it was too hard and too boring. After I discovered I could find pretty rocks on hikes, it became more like a treasure hunt. When I was ten, my father took me on my first overnight hike. My grandfather loaned me his copy of John Muir's, *The Mountains of California,* and it was then that I began to appreciate and fall in love with hiking and the mountains.

Friends increased my interest in the outdoors. My neighborhood friend Donna led the other children in outdoor adventures. My favorite was the fort we built after Christmas each year with old Christmas trees.

It helped that the families of two of my junior high friends had cabins near Fallen Leaf. My friend Margaret's family's cabin was only a mile from Fallen Leaf so the two families took a lot of hikes together. They included a two-week burro trip on the Muir Trail when I was sixteen.

When I was eight years old I wanted to become a writer but my mother told me that writers make very little money. When I began to win ribbons in the local science fair for my rock collection, I decided to be a geologist instead. I also thought it would be fun to be a forest ranger because rangers got to spend all their time in the mountains. At a high school career day, I discovered that girls could not be forest rangers and during my first week at Stanford, my faculty advisor told me that women geologists were hired only as curators of fossils. He also told me that there was only one other woman who majored in geology at Stanford. I was too shy to think that I could fight the system, so after that year, I switched to biology. I began to work at mountain resorts in the summers and during the school year, I climbed with the Stanford Alpine Club.

My interest in mountains and my lack of confidence affected my relationships with young men. On and off for two years, I dated a young man from the Alpine Club in whom I had no romantic interest but I thought I should because he enjoyed the mountains. At the same time, the first summer I worked at a resort, the Stanford Sierra Camp at Fallen Leaf, I dated a fellow employee. But that relationship only lasted for two months.

That same summer I had met another young man, Wayne, when he came up to visit friends. He had given me a wild ride over to Tahoe to meet my Alpine Club friend. We saw each other on campus often and, eventually, he asked me out. We were married during the summer between my junior and senior years.

Our first child, Doug, was born before I completed the classes I needed to graduate so I had to study and take the finals later. It was hard for me to adjust to an infant. Even though I had babysat, I had not realized that babies cried so much and Doug was no exception.

The same year that Doug was born, I was offered a teaching assistantship for the following year but I had to turn it down. We had no money for me to go to graduate school and besides, I thought that women with children were supposed to stay home with them or they would turn out bad.

When Doug was one year old, Wayne graduated from law school and we moved to Boise where he worked for a law firm. I liked Idaho but I was homesick for my family and friends and for Fallen Leaf. My homesickness became worse when I heard that my Fallen Leaf friend Margaret and her sister Carrie had been killed in a car accident. Margaret's death showed me that there is no guarantee that the people we are fond of would always be around. Later that summer, when Wayne took Doug and me camping in the Sawtooth Mountains, I felt less homesick because I had found new lakes and mountains to substitute for Fallen Leaf.

After eighteen months in Boise, we moved to Caldwell, just before our daughter Leslie was born. Wayne became the deputy prosecutor for Bill Brauner for two years and then started a law practice with him that lasted for several years.

In the summers, Wayne went to army reserve camp for his two-week vacation. This bothered me because when I was a child, the family vacation had been the best time of the year. To alleviate my disappointment, I often took Doug and Leslie and later Neal, Hilary and Stuart down to Fallen Leaf to visit my parents while Wayne was at camp.

A couple of years after we moved to Caldwell, I read an article about a Forest Service cabin area in the Sawtooths forty miles north of Sun Valley. The article made me want to get a lot there and build our own cabin. That Labor Day weekend we drove up to the Sawtooths and picked a lot with a beautiful view. Two years later Wayne dug and poured the foundation. Five years after that he built the outside of the cabin, and for nine more years the whole family worked to finish the inside.

I remember once when I took the children to the cabin a few days before Wayne's vacation. I was determined to take a hike with the kids before Wayne came up to join us. I managed to drive the primitive Hell Roaring Road, even though we got stuck in the creek for a while, and I managed to get the kids to hike the two miles to Hell Roaring Lake. Doug was thirteen, Leslie ten, Neal seven, Hilary four, and Stuart two. When Wayne arrived we went to Hell Roaring again because it was the only good hike for small children that I had found by then.

In August 1971, we took the children on our first pack trip. We took three riding horses for the seven of us so the younger children would not have to walk much. Although Wayne and Doug got bucked off, and the horses ran away at lunch one day, we made it from Pettit Lake to Redfish in five days with the help of our outfitter, Max Bitton, and his son Jeff.

After seeing the slow progress we were making on the cabin, I reached the conclusion that the cabin would be completed a lot faster if I got a job to help pay for it. I began taking classes to get a teaching credential because teaching would give me a long summer vacation for mountain hikes with the family.

In the spring of my first year back at school, surgery for a slipped disk made me fear I might never be able to hike again. When I found I could hike after all and saw a hiking guidebook for the Cascades in Washington, I got the idea of writing a hiking guidebook for the Sawtooths and White Clouds. That fall, as I continued my classes, I began writing up some of the hikes I had taken.

The next spring I saw a poster at the College of Idaho (Albertson College) for a booklet published by the college's Snake River Regional Studies Center describing twelve hikes in the Owyhees and Seven Devils. Thinking they might publish my book, I went to see the director of the center, Donna Parsons. She agreed to edit the manuscript after I added some more hikes that summer. That fall she insisted I send out letters and sample chapters to forty publishers. None of the publishers wanted to do my book but I kept hiking and backpacking to increase the number of hikes described in the book. Perhaps the most difficult was the three-day trip into the Boulder Chain Lakes in the White Clouds with Hilary and Stuart when they were eight and six. During the hike, I was usually carrying one of their packs as well as mine. It was lucky I took only two sleeping bags for the three of us or we never would have made it.

I earned my teaching credential but the only jobs I could find were substituting and temporary teaching. A stabbing incident by one of the sixth grade students helped me to realize that I really did not like teaching at all. I loved children and the subjects I taught but keeping an orderly class was difficult.

By the time I finally found a publisher in 1977, the cabin had running water and indoor plumbing.

That same year, the Sawtooth National Recreation Area officials agreed to let their chief wilderness ranger, Dave Lee, edit my book for accuracy. He urged me to include fifteen rarely used trails. That summer I managed to do all of them, nine in one twelve-day stretch, alternating kids so as not to wear them out.

Trails of the Sawtooth and White Cloud Mountains was supposed to come out in 1978 but my publisher sold the company, which delayed it a year. Once the book came out, Lou Florence, the owner of a mountaineering shop in Boise, encouraged me to give slide shows to civic groups. The questions asked at these shows inspired me to write another guidebook.

I have had many adventures while doing research for my books. The most difficult hike was when Doug, Stuart and I hiked down Big Creek to the Middle Fork of the Salmon and up to the raft-launching site at Dagger Falls. It was June and the water rose unexpectedly. When rapids covered the trail, we were forced to turn back. Luckily, the caretaker at the Taylor Ranch on Big Creek was able to radio the mail pilot and arrange for him to pick us up and drop us off on the Middle Fork above the worst of the high water.

The hiking guidebooks I have written include *Trails of the Sawtooth and White Cloud Mountains, Trails of Western Idaho, Trails of the Frank Church–River of No Return Wilderness,* and with co-author Jerry Painter, *Trails of Eastern Idaho.* I have also written three books of natural history, *Mountains* and *Forest Fires,* both published by John Wiley & Sons of New York, and with co-author Betty Derig, *Wild Berries of the West.*

I haven't made enough to live on with my writing and the walking has worn away the cartilage in some of my joints, but it has been rewarding to earn money for what I love to do . . . hike.

Mildred Tillotson

"Bloom where you are planted."

I was born during the Depression in 1929. I was the youngest of four children. My siblings were fourteen months apart and six years older, so I was raised as if I was an only child.

Mother was a single parent and believed that her place was at home with her children. We lived on three acres of pasture, which had a house, garage, chicken coop and shop. Mother rented the land to a local doctor to use for his dairy cows. We raised chickens and ducks. Mother gardened our own and the neighbor's land in order to feed and clothe us. My uncle used the shop for his blacksmith trade and my grandfather built a room for himself in the garage where he lived most of the year. Occasionally, he would pack his valise and take the train to Shoshone to visit his other children. Grandpa always brought us horehound candy upon his return. It was awful, but it was candy.

Chores were a big part of our lives. I weeded the gardens. My mother and brother milked the cows. Mother took in sewing and ironing. My sisters helped out with the cooking and cleaning.

I had an invisible friend. My sisters called her "Airy Mary." We'd play together and spend time dreaming in the sunshine under the old maple tree in the back yard. The tree continues to stand behind the bank building on Orchard Street.

I grew as Boise grew. During World War II, I got caught up in the excitement of Gowen Field. The buses full of young men would pass our home. My sisters would invite some of the young boys over every once in a while for an evening of fun and food. Mother would feed the young soldiers a home-cooked meal and I would wish that I were old enough to be a part of the thrill and for the boys to look at me differently than just as a little sister.

On Halloween night in my brother's senior year, a boy threw a stick at him and as a result he lost the sight of one eye. Mother was furious. She pulled my brother and sister out of Franklin High and immediately rented an apartment in town. She enrolled the two of them in St. Teresa's Catholic Academy. We lived in the Belgravia Apartments for more than a year until my brother and sister graduated. Then we moved back to the farm.

I started Franklin High in the fall of 1943. Our school dances were held at the Hotel Boise Crystal Ballroom. My dates hated to take me all the way home out on Orchard Road from downtown Boise.

After I graduated from St. Teresa's Academy I became a secretary. I worked for two years until I married my husband Tom. We were both born at St. Alphonsus Hospital and grew up within a mile of each other. I had known Tom as a child and became reunited with him after we had grown while he and his father were building a house on one of our family lots.

Tom and I had six children. I spent as much time as possible helping with the construction projects while keeping the children out of his way. I made meals for the crew and kept up with our own meals and projects around the house. So I was a busy lady.

The children attended Sacred Heart Elementary. The faculty, parents, and children were one big and happy family. We painted one another's houses, went camping, and enjoyed community projects together. We were a part of each other's lives then and continue to be today.

Our children and grandchildren continue to be the focus of Tom's and my life. Our eldest daughter Suzanna is a Family Therapist. Our son Dan has retired after serving twenty-one years in submarine service. He is now an engineer in nuclear waste and the father of three children. Our third son Tim was a helicopter mechanic. His life ended in a helicopter accident when he was twenty-eight years old. He made his mark in life with humor and zest. His daughter was only two months old when he died. She is now a beautiful young lady who celebrated her sweet sixteen this year. Bryan is the manager of a meat department for a grocery store. Jane is a hair stylist. She is the mother of two more of our grandchildren. Our youngest son Paul has inherited the family genes for music. He is a jazz pianist who divides his time between New York and Idaho. I love the diversity in our children. They are each a joy in our lives.

"Bloom where you are planted." I believe that my joyful life right here in Boise, Idaho, has represented this lovely statement. It is wonderful to be recognized as a long time member of this growing area. The little ones who I have sung with through the years come to me to renew friendships. I continue to sing and play with their little ones and we, the grandparents, reminisce with one another when we come together. There are many stories to tell and with each story, another memory flashes before me.

The graveled roads are now four-lane thoroughfares and my house on Orchard Road is gone. But Boise is where my heart stays as I visit other parts of the world. I am always assured that I will return to Boise with great joy and expectations for a new tomorrow and the memories I hold so dear.

Ruth Garrison

"I had complete confidence that I would succeed in whatever I tried to do if I just stuck with it long enough."

I was born on November 29, 1927, in Columbus, Ohio. I do not know where we were living at the time as my dad moved around a lot and we lived in various towns in central Ohio. I remember the names of London, Lancaster, and Westerville. My sister Miriam Louise (Mimmy Lou) was sixteen months older than I. My dad held various jobs; I remember he worked as an Omar bread man, delivering bread to the home. This is a fond memory because sometimes he had to cover two routes. He started on the second route just as I got home from school so I was able to go with him and ride in the Omar bread truck. I remember a large, white house with a wraparound porch. I was sick a lot and was not allowed to run and play like the other children. I remember sitting on the porch cutting out Katzenjammer Kids paper dolls. (This was a comic strip very popular at that time.) I also had a kitten, which I dressed in doll clothes and put in the baby buggy.

The Depression was a hard time as my dad was unable to find work so the family separated. My mother, my sister and I went to live with her parents in Circleville, Ohio, and my dad lived with his folks on a farm outside of town. This must have been a hard time for my parents but it was a fun time for me. My mother's folks were friendly, loving people; they lived in a large house with a large yard. Mother's younger brother, my Uncle Bob, lived there as well. Uncle Bob always had a surprise for me when I came down to breakfast. He also bought me ice cream cones and comic books, something my parents could not do. My dad came every Friday night and we always looked forward to his coming.

My dad finally got work and we moved, first to a house in Circleville and then to Westerville, Ohio. This is where I started school and stayed there through the fifth grade. It was a happy time in my childhood. I could walk to the open fields and wade through the shallow streams. Otterbein College is in Westerville and I saw my first Shakespeare, the "Midsummer's Night Dream." I did not understand much of it, but I still remember the magic of all those creatures.

But things did change. My dad started working for the state and we moved to the capital city of Columbus, Ohio. There was no open land, many people, cars and noise. My sister loved it but I never really adjusted to city living. I became claustrophobic and avoided crowds and noise. Consequently, I would walk miles rather than ride the crowded, noisy streetcars.

I also had experiences that have affected my life today. I was in junior high during World War II. There were strange people moving into the neighborhood and some of the children were in my school. I learned that these were refugees from Hitler's Europe and I became aware of the horror of their experiences. One girl who was a close friend all the way through college was the sole survivor of her family. One boy was said to have been in a Hitler Youth Group. Another family was on the last boat from Lithuania before the German U-boats closed the North Sea. Out of this came a strong determination to fight oppression and discrimination in any form. And this is my driving force today as I am a member of many human rights organizations.

I do not remember choosing a career. I was programmed to be a nurse. My mother's youngest sister was a nurse and I always admired her strength and independence. So I entered Ohio State University and received a Bachelor of Science in nursing degree. During this time Amos, the brother of my friend Jean Garrison, returned from the military and we were married in 1949. We both graduated at the same time in December.

I started to work at Grant Hospital, soon advancing to Head Nurse of an orthopedic, neurological, and psychiatric unit, which was quite a combination. Then Amos was transferred to Marietta, Ohio, and I decided not to work upon our arrival. But I soon was bored and started teaching Home Health Care for the American Red Cross.

The following year, our son, Paul Jackson, was born and two years later, our daughter, Carol Jean, came into this world.

When the children were in the primary grades we moved to Fremont, Ohio. Amos was traveling most of the time and the children were in school. I taught Sunday school, was Brownie leader for the Girl Scouts, Cub Scout leader for the Boy Scouts, and I started evening school in education. I had completed all requirements for teacher certification when Amos was transferred to Bloomsburg, Pennsylvania, and I stated teaching the fourth grade in a small rural school. After six years, we moved again, this time to Bozeman, Montana, where I felt that I had come home. We lived out of town, had horses and I could cross-country ski out my back door. I taught sixth grade science to 180 students each day and loved every minute of it.

But it did not last. Amos was transferred to Denver, Colorado, and a year later to Boise, Idaho. I decided to go back into nursing and worked for St. Luke's Hospital, now St. Luke's Regional Medical Center. After three years, I moved to the Veteran's Administration Medical Center and later retired from that facility.

During this time, I decided my husband wasn't going to be the only pilot in the family and I earned my private pilot, instrument and commercial ratings. I also earned a Master's of Education in Counseling from the College of Idaho, now Albertson's College. I passed the exam to become a Licensed Professional Counselor and had my own office for six years. When I reached seventy years young, I decided it was time to quit work, travel, volunteer, take swimming lessons and see what else there is that is exciting to do.

My mother used to say "Never go back, always make progress forward," and that is a good axiom to follow. I have always had complete confidence that I would succeed in whatever I tried to do if I just stuck with it long enough.

Mary Jenkins

"There goes that little old lady, working so hard to be a golfer."

I was born eighty years ago in Hailey, Idaho, twelve miles south from those famous ski slopes at Sun Valley.

I have been married for fifty-eight years. We did not have children, but I do have three grandnieces and one grandnephew, the grandchildren of my only brother who died last year.

I grew up in Boise during the Depression.

All through elementary and high school and on to junior college in Boise, my teachers were poorly paid but very dedicated. They taught the students well. I absorbed a lot by developing good study habits, which in turn became good work habits when it came time to earn a paycheck.

In June of 1939, I graduated from Boise Junior College and the Boise AAUW Chapter gave me a scholarship for $250 to the University of Idaho. I decided to get a Bachelor's Degree in Liberal Arts with a minor in Journalism. The summer before college was to start, I learned about a job opening on the staff of the *Boise Capital News,* the town's evening newspaper. I applied but was turned down by the editor. He didn't want to hire a girl.

Discouraged, I walked home. But as I walked into our front door the phone rang and Mother told me that the editor wanted me to return to the office. He had changed his mind and I became a proof-reader. My starting wage was $18 a week. I told the AAUW that I would not be using the scholarship. I said that I would go to college at a later date. The person I spoke to smiled and said, "You never will." She was right.

Instead, I launched a 45-year career in Boise journalism, starting on the proof desk in a cubbyhole that was no bigger than my clothes closet at home. But I didn't care because I was working on a newspaper and I never wanted to do anything else. I wasn't interested in public relations, television, free-lancing and certainly no plot for a novel was lurking in my brain. I was just where I wanted to be. And I stayed until I retired.

Three years after I was hired to work for the *Capital News,* it was sold to *The Idaho Statesman.* I went along with the furniture.

When World War II began, the men, including my husband left for the armed services. My first assignment with *The Idaho Statesman* involved a move to Nampa to run the news bureau there for a year. Each evening I traveled back to Boise and wrote weather reports, obituaries and police reports. I worked from eight to midnight, often seven days a week, with a base pay of $40 a week. I was so happy that I never thought that perhaps a man in the same position would be making twice my income.

When the war was over and the GIs returned to their jobs, I was sent across the room to the Society/Women's department. It never occurred to me to object. If the women's liberation movement was abroad in the land, it hadn't touched me.

Through the years the department's name changed. "Family Living," "Features," "Daybreak," and "Life" were the new named sections. But I stayed put until September 1, 1984, when I turned 65 and it was time to go.

Some of the "ups" of the profession are as follows:

Attending the food editors' conferences in New York, Boston, Chicago, and San Francisco.

Staying over to see Joel Gray on Broadway in "Cabaret."

Watching the New York Yankees play the Pittsburgh Pirates in a World Series game in Yankee Stadium.

Back in Boise, there was a personal thrill in 1973 when the Idaho Press Women gave me their Woman of the Year award at their annual convention.

The stories I did every Christmas season for forty years always included the invitation to *Statesman* readers to supply gifts for the elderly in Boise Convalescent Homes. We published the list of requests from those in need and the public responded generously.

The newspaper started the project during the 1920s. My first assignment was in 1945 when Ada County Hospital was the only facility in the area that cared for the elderly. Through the years, the facilities requesting needed items grew and high school students offered their help. Then the Soroptimist Club of Boise came along and offered its members' services. They did such a great job that they are now in charge and *The Statesman* helps them.

Even though the job was full of "ups," as in any job there are always the "downs."

I remember how nervous I felt in the presence of Pat Nixon, who had accompanied her husband to Boise during his first run for the

presidency. She kept watching my note taking. I asked here if she helped her husband with his speeches. She smiled and said, "If you will put your pen away, I will tell you how he will talk to the people after he is elected." She continued, "You are old enough to remember FDR's radio fireside chats, aren't you?"

I replied with a smile and a "yes."

"Well, my husband can talk just as informally on television," she said.

At first I wondered why she didn't want this in print. Then it came to me. Here was a noted Republican adopting the speaking style of a legendary master of the art and a Democrat at that.

Then there was the frustrating experience with Ann Landers. She had been invited to Boise by *The Statesman* publisher to give her views on adolescent behavior to high school students across the city. Since she was a celebrity, I asked to interview her.

"Sorry," was the reply, "Miss Landers doesn't give interviews."

"That is nonsense," I thought. "We run her column all the time," I complained. "Why can't we talk to her in person?"

My complaint landed downstairs at the publisher's door. He sent word upstairs that if I was at *The Statesman* front doors the following morning at eight, I could sit in the back seat of his car and talk to Miss Landers as he drove her from one school to another. But the story had to be about what she said to the students.

There was another stipulation. She had to see the story before it was printed. I was taught that was a reporter's "no-no."

The next morning, I gave him a copy of the story. He handed it to Miss Landers on the way to the airport; she read it on the plane, called him from the Denver airport and said that it was fine. Two weeks later, I received a note from Miss Landers complimenting me on my accuracy.

I never liked to write about medical procedures. I stumbled over the terminology. I was always at a loss for words when it came to describing a bereaved widow or parent.

Sometime in the 1970s, personnel changes were being made in the editorial department. A young generation of college graduates, some with a Master's degree, was taking over. For several months I had been running our department, known informally as the "Goodwill Department" because we helped local organizations with their civic projects. Then, suddenly, I was not running anything and the young man who replaced me was not about to help anybody.

Everybody thought that I would leave in a huff but I didn't. My ego was hurt but I still wanted to be on the staff. And that attitude turned out to be right.

I learned to use the video display terminal, filed my stories on time, watched the changes being made and kept my mouth shut. I didn't want to be the old bag in the corner, always saying, "We've never done it that way."

Through the years, the younger generation became my friends. In fact, to them I was a valuable asset because many of them were newcomers to the area and knew nothing of local history or geography.

"Just what is the Boise Bench?" someone asked me one day.

Back in my freshman Psychology class at Boise Junior College, the students graded each other on personal traits. I scored high on perseverance. To me that means to stay with the job until it is done, don't be a quitter, try to do it better, give it your best shot.

And now that I am eighty you would think that I would be easing up a bit but I don't and probably never will.

My number one source of recreation, in fact it is a passion, is the game of golf. I have been at it for years, always with the desire to improve my swing and my putting. In the summer, I usually arrive at the course at six in the morning while it is still cool, not to play but to practice.

Everyone at the course who works early in morning knows me by now. The men in the pro shop, the bag boys, and the sandwich maker in the café all say "hello" as I pass by. They smile, but I know what they are thinking when I start for the practice range with a basket of balls in one hand and a couple of clubs in the other:

"There goes that little old lady, working so hard to be a golfer."

Ruby Gould

"I try to thank God everyday for all of my blessings, and in my eighty-one years of living, there have been many."

I was born in Gate City, Oklahoma, to my parents Myron and Lela Lamm Holton. I was named Ruby May. I joined one sister and two brothers, which eventually became six sisters and five brothers. My father delivered six of us.

We were a happy family with the usual teasing and squabbling. We moved often and I was in six different schools during my grade school years. We lived in one location for one year. That was the longest stay. Sometimes we walked the three miles to school, but Dad usually took us on horseback when the weather was bad. One place where we lived there were ten students in the whole school and half of them were family.

I went to high school in Vale, Oregon, for one year. My parents did not like the public school system but did not have enough money for an academy. So they opted to remove me altogether.

During this time, I helped mother keep house, and we canned hundreds of quarts of vegetables, meat and fruit. Apples, gleaned from orchards, and many bushels of potatoes with other storable vegetables were kept in our cellar.

When I was seventeen, I met and married Judson Gould. We moved to a farm of 160 acres. We had a small house without electricity or water. There was no bathroom, just a path, and a washtub for bathing. We carried our water from a neighbor's home.

I was twenty-one when our first son was born. We named him Milan, and he was followed 15 months later by another son, Bert, then two daughters, Judy and Sherrel.

By then we had water and electricity in the house. We also had a refrigerator and electric stove. In 1948, we moved to Middleton, Idaho, where we purchased 80 acres. We lived in a chicken house for the remainder of winter. Snow blew through the cracks. We had four children by then. We made bunk beds and cooked on a little heating stove. We made it that winter without any bouts of cold or flu. In the spring, we began building our home; we finished the basement and lived there until the completion. Judson farmed, worked in construction and at the Sugar Factory, and the last eleven years before he retired, at the J.R. Simplot Company in Caldwell. The children learned to work at an early age and all have done well. I am proud of them.

When we moved to Middleton, we joined the Baptist church and attended faithfully. All of my children, grandchildren, and — in June 2000 — my eldest great-grandchild graduated from Middleton High School.

In 1949, I was hired at the J.R. Simplot Company Food Division in Caldwell, where I worked the midnight shift for the first year and then was transferred to the day shift. I had short winter runs for a few years until I started working year-round on the packaging lines, both wholesale and retail. A job opening was available in the Cafeteria and I worked there until I heard the Print Shop had an opening. I was interviewed and hired by Lorry Roberts, the manager of the department. I worked in the darkroom developing and printing photos as well as assisting in the bindery. We built a fine friendship, but in 1976 I had to retire due to an unexpected surgery and a lengthy recovery.

Judson retired a year later. We purchased a twenty-five foot RV and travelled for eleven years, spending time in Arizona and California, a few months each year before Judson's health started failing. The last year required frequent transfusions and he died on March 11, 1988. He was seventy-two. We had been married for fifty-two years and were lucky to have had eleven years of retirement together.

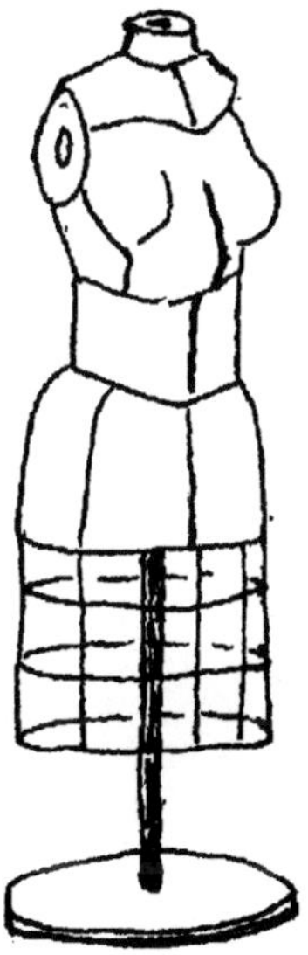

My hobbies have been many, but always centered around art: ceramics to oil painting and now china painting. I loved to sew and made all my kids' clothes when they were young. I designed wedding gowns for two of my daughters and two of my granddaughters.

My mother lived to the grand old age of 97 and one half. In March 1960, we girls had a slumber party for her birthday. We had so much fun that we continue this yearly ritual with mothers to granddaughters. Of the ten siblings still living, five are over eighty. We continue to share good times, lots of laughter and great discussions. My mother taught me to do unto others as I would have them do unto me. This has been a good rule for me to follow. I try to thank God every day for all of my blessings, for there have been many.

I look in the mirror through the eyes
of the child that was me.

— Judy Chicago

Lorraine Hosac

"If a woman chooses to bring a child into this world,
her first responsibility is to that child.
One of the most satisfying accomplishments
in life is a successful child."

I was the third of seven children born to Louis L. and Maud A. Barton Thomas on February 7, 1923. I lived in Fort Worth, Texas, from birth until our move to Carlsbad, New Mexico, in 1929. We lived in Carlsbad for three years. It was there that my father developed one of the first Public Health Laboratories and set up standards for health and cleanliness in restaurants and schools.

In 1932, when I was nine, we returned to Fort Worth, but not for long. Soon after our arrival back, father took us to Medicine Lodge, Kansas. We lived in Medicine Lodge for several years. Then, when I was in the eighth grade, we came to Idaho on the Union Pacific railroad. I went to junior and senior high school in Idaho, then on to the College of Idaho in Caldwell. The year was 1940 when I entered college. I graduated in 1944 with a degree in both Chemistry and Mathematics.

I married Chet Hosac during my second year in college. Our daughter was born the following year. Then three sons followed. So the educational years were busy years for me.

One of the most profound lessons of my life was to learn the importance of a goal. A goal influences an individual's decision. My goal as a student was to become a high school Chemistry teacher. However, goals continually change as our lives unfold and our attitudes and opportunities vary. But even with a changing goal, a pattern has been set and a certain amount of discipline has been achieved. Since my children were born when I was quite young, my goals were altered to fit. I did not work full-time after college, during their growing years. Working mothers were not too popular after World War II but I did substitute in the Boise Schools occasionally. I also taught piano lessons at home. While the children were in elementary school, I did my share of Boy Scouts, Girl Scouts, helping out at school, baking cookies and candies for school activities.

But eventually I became so bored that my husband agreed that I could go to work. I interviewed at the Idaho State Department of Health Laboratories and went to work as a microbiologist and chemist. I stayed at the laboratory for thirteen years, until I got too busy with my home life to have time to work. I resigned and again I changed my life. My goals by this time had been blended with my husband's who had gone into land development.

During the next twenty years, my husband and I developed property and traveled extensively. We were one of the early snowbird couples traveling with a travel trailer. During this time, we watched as our children finished their education, married, and had families of their own.

I felt during these years that there was no obstacle that could not be overcome. As a child during the Depression, I watched my parents live through hardships without the benefits of any government agencies. These experiences taught me that each person must contribute and do their share of the work. I believe the only way that a marriage can survive is if both people do their chores without fail.

As a sophomore in college during World War II, I witnessed every able-bodied male student leave the campus to enlist and fight for our freedom. I spent three years taking care of my daughter and waiting for my own husband to return. I saw my sister and my friends suffer through widowhood with no real proof of a death. This was also the period when women were finally accepted into the work force. The jobs women held were one of the ways to keep sane. It was difficult to start over again when the men returned after such a long separation. The war pushed many marriages to the limit.

My generation learned that we had to provide for ourselves and for our children. If a woman chooses to bring a child into this world, her first responsibility is to that child. One of the most satisfying accomplishments in life is a successful child. This is a great joy and all other efforts must take second place. I have been lucky.

If you associate enough with older people who do enjoy their lives, who are not stored away in any golden ghettos, you will gain a sense of continuity and of the possibility for a full life.

— Margaret Mead

Wilma Barry

***"It is important to have good family relationships,
be active in your church and community,
and never do anything to hurt anyone."***

William Lester Brink and Lillie Agnes Nelson Brink are Wilma's parents. Wilma is married to Lyle Theodore Barry, my grandpa. Wilma is the youngest of her family. She has three sisters and one brother. Her sisters' names are Alice, Mina and Dorothy. Alice and Dorothy are both deceased. I haven't met any of her family except for Mina. Mina lives in Albuquerque, New Mexico. I met her during a family vacation. Grandma's brother's name is Ivan. He too is deceased.

Wilma and Lyle have three children. The oldest is Jean Marie who lives near Boise, Idaho. She has one child name Joshua. Her husband Warren Greaves is a scuba diver, like my grandpa. They have made trips to Truk, Guam, Palau, Cozumel, Hawaii, Cabo San Lucas, the Great Barrier Reef and Key West. Grandma always joins them, but she finds other fun while the two men scuba dive.

My Uncle Lee is their middle child. He lives in San Lorenzo, California. Lee and his wife have three children. Lee also scuba dives.

My mom is Linda. She is Wilma and Lyle's youngest child. She and my dad, Michael Clark, have two daughters. My sister Rachel Jean is the oldest. I am their youngest daughter and my name is Amber Lee.

When Wilma was a child, she lived on a farm outside of Meridian, Idaho. Her father was a cattle buyer. Her mother worked in the packing shed during the fall. The family moved into town the year she started first grade. They didn't have kindergarten in those days.

I asked my grandma about her school memories. She told me that her favorite grade was the eighth because in eighth grade, you are the big shots. My grandma's best school memory was her valedictorian speech at the eighth grade graduation. Her worst school memory was at a Halloween dance when one of her classmates slid across the gymnasium floor and went through a window and gashed his arm. Her dearest friends were Marilyn, Betty Jo, Dorothy and Doris. Doris died of cancer, but Grandma keeps in touch with Doris' daughter, who resides in Boise.

Grandma's favorite movie is *My Friend Flicka* and her favorite book is *Little Women.* Her favorite song is " When the Deep Purple Falls." When my grandma was young, they didn't have television. Instead, she listened to the radio. Her favorite radio show was "Fibber McGee and Molly." Grandma loves to play card games like cribbage and pinochle. Her favorite car is a Chevrolet.

One of the most important places in my grandma's life was the old St. Alphonsus Hospital because all three of her children were born there. The other place that is important is the house she lives in now. That is because she and Grandpa have lived there since 1958.

My grandpa's family lived in the nearby town of Nampa but his father had a service station in Meridian. Grandpa worked there for his dad. When Grandma met him, she was fifteen and he was twenty-two. They were married June 4, 1950, when Grandma was eighteen and

Grandpa was twenty-five. They celebrated their golden anniversary in the year 2000.

Grandma had great admiration for Eleanor Roosevelt. Her favorite movie stars were Gregory Peck and Ingrid Bergman. Her favorite singers are Bing Crosby and Rosemary Clooney. Senator Frank Church and President Franklin Delano Roosevelt were her ideal politicians. Her sports heroes were Roger Maris and Mickey Mantle.

My grandma has had several jobs. She worked as a payroll clerk for the telephone company and as an accounts receivable clerk for the neighborhood drugstore. She was also the audit supervisor at Sears. At the age of 47, she enrolled in Boise State University. She worked full-time at Sears while earning her Bachelor's Degree in Accounting. She was a Certified Public Accountant for ten years, retiring in 1984. The best parts of all her jobs were the people she worked with and the worst part was getting up early every day.

In grade school, she played on the softball and volleyball team. She has enjoyed jet skiing for the past several years. She does aquatics for exercise. Her hobbies and interests are reading, knitting and genealogy. Grandma has always been active.

My grandma has been a Soroptimist since 1979. She has worked on many of their local projects. She has attended many regional, federation and international conventions. She feels a service club such as Soroptimist International is the best way to give back to your community and to make good friends all over the world.

Wilma's favorite holiday is Christmas because she receives many cards and letters from friends and relatives. Her favorite tradition is sending cards on all of the holidays to her grandchildren and great-grandchildren. My grandma considers television the greatest invention because there are so many educational features and a lot of entertainment. And because one can hear and see what is going on in the entire world.

My grandma's great-grandfather, Joshua Brink, was a great influence on her because he was a wonderful family man who took an interest in others. She thinks it is a lot of fun to be a grandparent because you can spoil your grandchildren rotten, including me, and send them home.

My grandma's advice for children of today is the following, "It is important to have good family relationships, be active in your church and community, and never do anything to hurt anyone."

Wilma's granddaughter, Amber Lee Clark, wrote this life story at the age of thirteen. She is now sixteen years old.

Julie Kreiensieck

"I fought the stereotype of a gray-haired woman for twelve years."

I was born in Boise, Idaho, on December 22, 1925. As an only child, my goal was to drive a logging truck pell-mell down the mountain roads. My father was born in Boise in 1884; he was in the police department several years, working the beat in Chinatown and the red light district. Mother was a teacher, drama person and activist.

The iceman used to come to the Arnolds' home behind us and could always be counted on to give a sliver of ice to a hot kid. There was open access to an artesian well in the Boise Cold storage building. On a hot evening, we sometimes went there — the room was so cool — and my mother really liked the water. On the Fourth of July, I remember little yellow ducks we put in a filled washtub and lit a wick in their tails and they putted around the water.

I entered the seventh grade at Washington Junior High, the first year it was open. After high school, I drove truck around Gowen Field for one year for the United States Army Air Corps. This is where I met M/Sgt. Charles Kreiensieck. My correspondence with Chuck paid off when he came home on furlough. We married in Boise a few weeks later. There wasn't much time for the family and friends to put on a formal wedding. We spent a few days in Sun Valley, Idaho, which was new and ritzy in 1947. From there we flew to Fairbanks, Alaska, where Chuck was stationed. Chuck was then transferred to Denver, Colorado. We had two daughters and I became a housewife.

I attended for two years Grinnel College in Iowa on a music scholarship. I love the flute and taught flute when the children were young. I still have a few students.

We left the service and moved back to Boise in 1953. Chuck got a job as a carpenter and we lived with my folks. Out of this came his acquaintance with the local building profession and he became a self-employed contractor. He and Dewey Bills started the Home Builders Association and the Parade of Homes. With the help of Sherm Perry Furniture, The Mode and others, I helped decorate the first three Parade of Homes that they built. I enjoyed that a lot. We had a third daughter and I helped with the business part of the company.

Around 1956, I became ill and my right leg was paralyzed. This was diagnosed as Iceland Disease (epidemic neuromyasthenia), which attacked my spinal column and affected my brain and emotions. I lost my memory and was often depressed and apathetic. I did physical therapy at the Idaho Elks Rehabilitation Hospital for five years. This was hard on the kids, Chuck, my parents and myself.

In the 60s there was a recession. Much of our assets were in spec houses and investment property. The bottom dropped out of the market and the company had to file bankruptcy. Chuck eventually went to Denver and to Kansas for awhile to help support us.

I found work as a clerk in the business part of the Boise Junior College library. The head librarian, Ruth McBirney, had faith I could do the job. There was a small staff so I got to learn many aspects of this field, working in acquisitions, purchasing, receiving, checking so as not to duplicate, and allocating funds. I started taking a class most semesters in Social Studies. I really liked my job and grew with it to become head clerk, even as I became active with some college issues. I finished my BA in Social Studies just as BJC became Boise State University.

At the same time I lost my home due to non-payment of taxes and moved back with my folks. My dad died not long after and Chuck came back to Boise. My sainted mother put up with us. Chuck left and we were divorced in 1971.

Through the Casey Family Program, I had two foster daughters — one at a time — and they were fifteen when they moved in. I thought I knew a lot about raising girls but I didn't know about abuse, lack of love, or lack of trust. It was a learning experience for all of us. During this time, I remodeled the house on Fifteenth Street; other kids came and went. There seemed to be a continual coming and going.

I worked one year after graduation but left and attended the University of Oregon in Eugene for three terms, earning my Master's in Library Sciences. I was class president for one term at age 48. I returned to Boise and, after a couple of false starts at jobs, I was hired by Morrison Knudsen in 1975. My mother had died in June of that year but she had succeeded in getting me educated.

Working for MK was somewhat of a culture shock. I had never considered my gender as an employment factor, but it was at MK. I had a staff of fifteen and we did a good job for the company, even though my job didn't exist before I was hired. I created a records management system, using computer-created microfilm for a central library of researching databases. This was corporate wide and the system still exists. I fought the stereotype of a gray-haired woman for twelve years before getting tired of having the fight.

I like to garden, I still teach flute and I love most music. I plan to stay productive and active in some way until I die. I figure the reason I am here on earth is for my soul, my mind, my being, to learn to love. To get an inkling of what the word means, look at God as love. If we are all part of God, we are part of total love.

Frances Long

"The value of this day is impossible to measure, for it will never come again."

Frances Long was born in Grand Rapids, Michigan, to Walter Jacob and Minnie Myrtle Long. Barbara Oldenburg writes that Frances "sang at an early age and remembers leading the singing in her first grade classroom. Her family moved to Boise when she was sixteen years old." She wanted to be a home economist but "she became well-known and much in demand as a soloist among the Boise Valley churches," as well as for PTA meetings, weddings, funerals and other occasions. "She was chosen to sing soprano lead in 'Chimes of Normandy' during her years as a music student at St. Margaret's School under Bernice Brusen."

Frances graduated from St. Margaret's High School, and received her BA from the College of Idaho. Oldenburg writes that Frances's additional "educational background includes attendance at the Cincinnati Conservatory of Music, and the Universities of Michigan, Idaho, Portland and California.

"Her teaching career began in 1930, in a one-room schoolhouse which is now the Murphy Museum. In 1931, she became teacher and principal for two years at Valley View School, then teacher and principal for two years at Maple Grove, grades five through eight. She next taught at Cole Elementary School for twelve years." Oldenburg writes that after Frances taught at "Campus Elementary for one year, she was appointed Primary Supervisor for the Boise Public School by Henry Von Der Heide, a position she held for sixteen years, until retirement in 1969.

"Frances was a member of the National Education Association, and a member and director of the first Presbyterian Church Choir. She served as President of the Soroptimist Club and was twice 'Woman of the Year.' She was President for two years of Delta Kappa Gamma (international honorary teachers' sorority), an officer in Chapter AT of PEO Sisterhood, and has belonged to several garden clubs."

Oldenburg writes that Frances managed a tea room and a gift shop in her home for two years, worked on the United Fund Drive and the Community Concert Membership Drive, taught Adult Education classes in classroom music for the University of Idaho, and was director of music for Job's Daughters.

"Frances Long was named 'Idaho Music Teacher of the Year' for 1967. In 1970, the All-School Music Week Program was dedicated to her and a Certificate of Appreciation was presented from the Boise Independent School District for thirty-five years of faithful and meritorious service. In March of 1976, she was honored by *The Idaho Statesman* as a 'Distinguished Citizen' and was proclaimed 'Soroptimist of the Year' in 1978."

Frances Long once said, "The value of this day is impossible to measure, for it will never come again. What I do is up to me and no one else. I can use it to good advantage or I can squander it away. The choice is mine."

In closing, Oldenburg adds that "Frances truly dedicated her life to teaching, to music, and to helping make life easier and happier for those around her. Her students, whether young or old, were always happy to be part of her classes. Boise is most grateful for the sharing of her musical talents and her wonderful sense of humor. We are all richer for having known and worked with her."

Cora Frances Long died at her home on Thursday, September 16, 1999, at the age of ninety-one.

Environment, in all its forms and relations, sustains us. We depend upon it. I truly believe that the fundamental principles of ecology govern our lives, wherever we live, and that we must wake up to this fact or be lost.

— Karin Sheldon

Mary Trail

"Following where the trail leads."

In this year 2000, I am again on the sage hills above the farmland where my maternal grandparents settled in 1900. It is the farm where my mother was born and where she lived until her death in April at age eighty-eight.

I haven't always lived in this valley as she did. My dad is a Trail and I think there is a bit of nomad in that line of farmers. I did begin here, however, sixty years ago, having the mysterious fortune of being born in Oregon, across the Snake River from the farm where I lived until I graduated from Payette High School in 1957.

That fall I moved to Arizona where I attended college, worked and adventured during the years of travel to and from Idaho. I earned two degrees from Arizona State University in Sociology. I applied my knowledge in jobs such as statistician, social worker and manager of a social service agency, particularly when I moved to Boise in the early 1970s.

The years seemed to skitter right along and I found myself closing my Boise career by serving a term on the Boise City Council (1981-

1986). Then, feeling called to live at "the beach," I worked and studied from a prime location in Cannon Beach, Oregon. During the summers, I returned to a little alley house in Ontario and was able to once again be a farm worker with my family.

My on-going job with the farm includes helping with the delivery of truck garden produce (corn, cantaloupes, watermelon, pumpkins and apples), errand running (*girls* on the farm are often the *gatherers*) and in autumn, my favorite time of year, apple harvest. I drive tractor in the orchards, which affords me the luxury of being outdoors with daily picnics for about six weeks.

During the winter of 1991, I walked the road on the sage hill above the apple orchard often. I would see coyote, deer, hawk, eagle, junco and magpie. The view into Oregon and up and down the Snake River Valley was beautiful in almost any mood of weather.

The next spring, a house on that hill became available and on June 1, 1992, I moved in, returning to reside where my girlhood roots are. Here I live with four dogs, two cats, five tanks of fish, and many trees, roses and other shrubs and lots of budding wisdom.

Today, ten days before my sixty-first birthday, I sense recognition of the wise choice to return to a rural area with access to small towns. Today is Monday, which means that I tended my house early, loaded my Blazer with fifty dozen ears of corn that I delivered to a couple of congenial women at a produce market on the north edge of Weiser. Then I drove toward town, gathering a Mocha at the Irish Mist Coffee stand, crossed the street, filled the vehicle tank with fuel, checked the "Wild Card' ticket (Sorry, not a winner, of course, I know better) and proceeded into town.

I went to the Les Schwab store where I had the tires rotated, paid the business bill, chatted with the bookkeeper telling her that local corn had been delivered (she will be a customer before the day is over) and received the information that the front brake pads are severely worn. I asked for an estimate with intention of getting a second opinion. (Now that is elder wisdom, not to allow such diagnoses to throw one into a panic).

From there I went around the downtown construction (no traffic jam, no delay) to the Post Office where the clerk greeted me with a friendly "hello." I had a parcel addressed to Gila, New Mexico. He said, "Heela, or is that Gilla, you know, as in La Golla, California." I could only laugh.

Yes, insurance. After all, the box had clip-on earrings from the collection of an eighty-eight year old Crone friend of mine who was willing to share with the women of today who want to dress "retro." I think that means 1950s and before. Yes, stamps as I am still writing notes of gratitude to those who remembered my mother with charitable contributions. He brought out a full page of stamp options and told me what he had. I chose the roses, rainforest animals and tropical flowers. No one was behind me grumping about my deliberative process, either.

Soon I was out the door and across the street to the accountant's office where I left some estate information and picked up material he had been compiling.

Around the corner to the Idaho Bag Company, where I ordered a bale (or maybe two, I wasn't sure and it didn't make any difference) of 500 burlap bags which are used for marketing the corn. The "Bag Lady," a lovely Japanese-American woman,

called me Mary. I see her only once a year and haven't yet remembered *her* name.

With my errands done, I went to the farmhouse, tended the vegetable garden and returned to my home on Sage Hill at about 11:30 to give my dogs a thirty-minute romp before I started something else.

Yes, I am affirmed it was wisdom that brought me back to my roots where I am soul nourished.

Jane Wallich

"Keep your good sense of humor, laugh at yourself, keep a stiff upper lip, and meet the world with courage."

I was born June 10, 1918, at St. Alphonsus Hospital in Boise, Idaho. Jim Hopper, my brother, is five years younger. My father owned the Gem State Electric Company. My mother was a wonderful homemaker. My Aunt Nell Tragaskis, my mother's sister, was always good to me and her husband, Uncle Vern, also was great.

I started school at Washington Elementary on 15th Street in Boise. I went to high school at Boise High and then to Boise Junior College, now Boise State University. I continued my education at San Jose State College where I majored in music. I received a Bachelor of Art in Teaching.

We lived on North 15th Street in the house my dad and two uncles built after work at night. I always wanted my own room and, on my twelfth birthday, I moved into our new home on the same street. I had a bright pink bedroom all to myself.

I started teaching at King City, California in the spring after I graduated from college. While teaching, I met Walter Wallich who was in the service and stationed in a building in King City. He loved music and invited the people of King City to share their classical records at the United Service Organization (USO). I had played my cello for a group of business ladies.

Afterwards another teacher asked me if I would like to go to the USO to listen to records. After the record session, Walter asked me if he could carry my cello home. It was almost 11:00 and I knew that he had to be in at 11:00. I said, "Okay, but you don't know what you're getting into." I lived six long blocks away. He said, "I've carried cellos before and I don't mind the walk."

That episode led to a year of getting to know each other. We were married on June 6, 1943, in San Jose, California, at the Congregational Church.

We had planned to be married in Boise, Idaho, but Walter's furlough had been canceled. Mother rode the bus from Boise to King City for the wedding. My dad could not come because he had to wind a pump motor for the city of Weiser. Since it was wartime, there was no chance to buy a new pump so Dad was forced to stay behind and work. At the wedding, Walt and his buddy Mel realized that we did not have anybody to take Mother down the aisle so they rushed out and grabbed a soldier who was walking by the church. My best friend was my maid-of-honor. She and Mel married that fall before his company was shipped to New Guinea. Our husbands were gone for two long years.

After the wedding, a bouncy lady came out of the church and announced that everyone was invited to her home for cake and ice cream. We had over fifty friends. She had rice to throw and had made two cakes. That must have cost her a lot of red stamps. (Red stamps were sugar ration stamps during the war). When my mother asked her how we deserved such a nice party, she said, "Mrs. Hopper, you had my

son Jim out to dinner several times when he was stationed in Boise at Gowen Field. Also, Jane has always played her cello for us when we asked her." Mother said she never had bread and butter turned into cake and ice cream so quickly. It was a very special time.

I came home to Boise and taught the fourth grade at Longfellow school. I also taught music to the whole school.

Walt and I have two wonderful daughters who are married to two great husbands. Judi and Tom have children Peter and Patti. Mark and Jan have Amanda. Our children and grandchildren are the delight of our lives.

I was born with dislocated hips that caused me to be lame. I have always experienced a lot of pain. But I have had a wonderful life and have done everything everyone else did, except ride a horse and ski. Dad told me, "Keep your good sense of humor, laugh at yourself, keep a stiff upper lip, and meet the world with courage." And that's what I have done.

For years I collected bells and gave bell talks to the clubs in Boise. When the girls graduated from college, Walt gave me two sets of bells. My friend, Phyllis McClenahan, accompanied me on the piano. We enjoyed providing musical programs to various clubs and churches without charge. My daughter Judi is a music teacher. I recently gave her my bells for her students to enjoy.

I now belong to the Fortnightly Club (a study club founded in the 1890s), the American Association of University Women and the Congregational Church. Walt and I also volunteer at the Discovery Center of Idaho.

My goal is to enjoy Walt and our friends, and to have our friends and families enjoy me as well. Walt is a wonderful husband and has taken good care of me over the years. We aren't wealthy but we live a good life. How lucky can we be?

Scora Stump

"I guess you could say my career chose me."

When she first arrived in Boise, Scora Stump went to an employment agency and filled out an application. She had worked in restaurants back in Fort Hall and even had experience in managing such a place, doing things like bookkeeping and ordering supplies. She felt confident that she could find a job in a Boise restaurant. In the interview stage of her application, the man told her that all she could do was housekeeping. "I never went back to the employment agency."

Scora was born in 1930, in Fort Hall, Idaho, a small township on the Fort Hall Indian Reservation. She lived in a two-room structure — called a "bunkhouse" — with her father and mother and six siblings. They had no pets but her mother had a garden in which Scora loved to work, helping with the growing and picking and canning of the vegetables that they would eat through the winter.

In such a close-knit household, being good meant behaving and minding her parents and treating her siblings with respect. If her father called her name, "and he only called it once," she went immediately. Talking back, or not doing as she was told, was unthinkable in a household that worked solely to survive. There were no special jobs allotted to the children in the house. "If trash needed to be taken out, it was because the trash needed to be taken out."

Her father was the biggest source of inspiration in her life; he came up from Mexico to farm, migrating first to Montana and then to Idaho. Her mother followed two years later. Neither of them could speak English, but her father wanted his children to have an education and he sent them to school. The school Scora attended in Fort Hall was different from modern schools: each teacher taught two grades, so she had one teacher for the first and second grades, another for the third and fourth, and yet another for the fifth and sixth. The principal of the school taught seventh and eighth grades. The children rode the bus back and forth the twelve miles from Fort Hall to Blackfoot during high school. "It was the only means of transportation."

Even on and near the Indian Reservation, there was racial prejudice, though it was more often than not left unspoken. "There were certain places where we had to sit in movie theaters." In a day and age when there was no such labeling of groups as "majority" and "minority," she remembers it very vividly. "In Fort Hall, there was a majority of Indians, the middle class were Caucasians, and then there were Mexicans. In Blackfoot, there was a majority of Caucasians, then Indians and then Mexicans." She was also looked down upon because she was from the country and didn't live in the town of Blackfoot.

She married Marshal Stump, a white mechanic from the area, when she was 23 years old. Though "intermarriages" were not looked upon too favorably in the community, her parents approved of the marriage. Only one of her siblings, a sister, married someone of Mexican descent. Marshal and Scora moved to Boise in 1953.

Just like a job, finding a house was difficult. She would talk to people over the telephone with no trace of an accent in her voice. When she would go to look at the house, it was suddenly sold. "I remember one time when I was trying to buy a piece of property in Garden City. I talked to the realtor on the phone, and in the time it took him to hang up and meet me at the lot, the land had already been sold."

Due to the fact that she was a Mexican woman in the early 50s, the only job Scora could find was housekeeping, a job she held for 35 years. "I guess you could say my career chose me." She stayed with one family for twenty-six years, another for nineteen. Many of the people she worked for are still acquaintances of hers. Though she and her husband had no children of their own, Scora raised seventeen children at her various jobs. "I raised them as if they were my own family."

Scora likes gardening, sewing, embroidering, and crocheting. She has worked with the Veterans of Foreign Wars in the Canteen, reading bingo and such, and she was the Auxiliary president for five years. She is still active in her church; her father was very spiritual in faith as is she but did not go to church regularly. As for words of wisdom, Scora says, "Life is what you make it. You must have the determination to go after what you want."

Feminism called upon me to have the courage to grow up, to discover and exercise my womanly strength, to be unafraid of pain – and the pain is immeasurable – knowing that fully experienced, it makes joy fully possible.

— Sonia Johnson

Ila Greenfield

"His response to my note, 'We are out of fuel,' was 'So are we.' "

I was born in Wolsey, South Dakota, on a 2000-acre ranch. Our home had hot and cold running water and inside toilets. My mother had a hired girl and we had a number of hired men. Almost all of the local schoolteachers in our area lived with us, but the privilege carried a responsibility, as they — men and women — were required to work for their room and board.

My two brothers and two sisters and I were reared with a strong work ethic in an equally strong democratic setting.

Until the sixth grade, we attended the country school. Later, the schools were consolidated and we went to the city of Wolsey on the school bus. Our education was advanced compared to the students in Wolsey so my sister and I immediately moved up one grade upon entering the city school.

After I graduated from high school, I went into a rather dark world. The Depression had begun. My father managed to retain his ranch but he had very little money. Farm prices were at an all-time low. I remember that oats sold for only six cents a bushel.

In September, with enough money for tuition in my pocket and two suitcases, I hitchhiked to Aberdeen, South Dakota, where I enrolled at Northern State Teachers College. I received an associate degree in elementary education. While in college I was a member of the intramural championship basketball team and swimming team.

I don't recall any gender bias but after teaching three years, I was married and promptly lost my job. Married women teachers were not allowed to teach unless the husband could not find employment. This policy was due to the Depression.

Remembering those times is more painful than living through them. Maybe this is because everyone was living under the same conditions. I remember teaching in a two-room schoolhouse when we ran out of fuel. I sent a note home with the daughter of the president of the school board. His response to my note, which stated, "We are out of fuel," was "So are we."

The first time I voted, I supported Franklin D Roosevelt's second term. My political persuasion has never changed. Roosevelt was smart and he tried everything to end the nation's suffering. One of his measures sought to reduce supply, which could create higher farm prices. There was an oversupply of pork, which resulted in nearly six hundred pigs being killed on my father's ranch.

Political events have been important factors in my life. My father had a political appointment in South Dakota. When the Democrats lost the state elections in the late 1930s, we came to the West.

World War II began and families were separated. In 1946, I was a single mother with three children. I was forced to work. I was hired at Northwest Airlines in Spokane, Washington. World War II opened many new opportunities for women. I was able to obtain a loan and purchase a house.

In Spokane, there were two types of people, Republicans and Catholics. This was true at Northwest Airlines also. One of my duties was to sort through the messages from the airlines general office in St. Paul, Minnesota.

One day, in October 1948, a message came from the Vice President of sales in St. Paul, advising all employees to vote for Thomas E. Dewey for president as his platform reflected the philosophy and aspirations for the future of Northwest Airlines. To this day I can't believe that I responded to the message by telling the Vice President that I would vote for whomever I chose and that my freedoms as an American were being flagrantly violated.

Instead of receiving punishment for my actions, I received praise and soon I was the lead agent for Northwest.

Another political event that shaped my life occurred in 1958. I was with a group of Republicans at a private club in Spokane, defending Harry Truman. A gentleman who had been listening to the rather spirited conversation came to the aid of the lone Democrat. He was George Greenfield, the Democratic State Chairman from Idaho. Two years later, we were married and I moved to Boise, Idaho.

In 1966 I founded New World Travel in Boise. Being a travel agent has its rewards. George and I have visited over one hundred countries in the past twenty years. Each country we visited reinforced our appreciation for our own country.

Along with my travel career, I have been active in the community. I have been a member of Soroptimist International of Boise since 1968, and served two years as president. I have belonged to the Boise Chamber of Commerce and a group called the Gold Dusters, which helps establish new businesses in town. I have also been a very active member of the Downtown Boise Association.

After twenty-four years in business, I sold the travel agency in 1990, but not without Plan B. I gathered up the credits I had earned from the six colleges I had attended and enrolled in a master's program at Boise State University. After several years of hard work, I received a Master's Degree in History. I am now working on a degree in Art History. I am currently a volunteer at the Boise Art Museum.

I have no regrets about my professional life but I do regret that I did not spend more time with my children. My work was a requirement, but I think I could have spent a little less time on housekeeping.

I have been blessed with a long and wonderful life. The length of my life and the source of my physical strength are most likely related to my Scandinavian genes.

But, most importantly, I try to learn something new every day.

LIFE IS AN OPPORTUNITY: BENEFIT FROM IT

LIFE *is beauty; admire it*
LIFE *is bliss; taste it*
LIFE *is a dream; realise it*
LIFE *is a duty; complete it*
LIFE *is a game; play it*
LIFE *is costly; care for it*
LIFE *is wealth; keep it*
LIFE *is love; enjoy it*
LIFE *is a mystery; know it*
LIFE *is a promise; fulfill it*
LIFE *is sorrow; overcome it*
LIFE *is a song; sing it*
LIFE *is a struggle; accept it*
LIFE *is a tragedy; confront it*
LIFE *is an adventure; dare it*
LIFE *is luck; make it*
LIFE *is too precious; do not destroy it*
LIFE *IS* LIFE *; FIGHT FOR IT*

— Mother Theresa

Index
for Elder Tales

Shizue Abo 13
Dale Angers 59
Billie Baker 53
Sally Baker 135
Miriam Barr 9
Wilma Barry 237
LaRue Cheney 65
Bethine Church 33
Calla Cornwell 131
Sylvia Creek 141
Delores Crow 145
Luanne Crump 201
Helen Dagres 55
Mary Daley 29
Carol Dick 127
Alice Dieter 185
Dotage Party 205
Inez Dotson 207
Marge Formo 123
Maxine Freeman 47
Francelle Fritz 125
Margaret Fuller 209
Ruth Garrison 219
Ruby Gould 229
Ila Greenfield 261
Novella Hart 197
Ona Healy 137
Lorraine Hosac 233
Mary Jenkins 223
Jayne Jones 37
Eileen Keith 193
Julie Kreiensieck 241
Ruth Barnes Kunze 69
Alice Laan 83

Frances Long 245
Betty Luginbill 87
Margaret Martinez 101
Mary Milton 91
Velma Morrison 75
Dorris Murdock 107
Vera Noyce 79
Dr. Mamie Oliver 113
Clara Posey 111
Shirley Randolph 17
Loretta Reed 149
Lorry Roberts 117
Fern Lucille Sawyer 1
Esther Simplot 95
Lucille Smylie 157
Ardis Snyder 161
Ruby Stone 165
Susie Stoval 175
Scora Stump 257
Rachel Tanner 169
Helen Thomson 49
Mildred Tillotson 215
Mari Carmen Totorica 21
Mary Trail 249
Ann Vycital 179
Jane Wallich 253
Marilyn Watts 5
Jean Wilson 153
Adelaide Woodcook 25
Carmalita Zamzow 41

Is a family member included in this book?

Want a copy of your own?

A copy for the granchildren?

Yes, I want to have a personal copy of this book.
Please send me _____ copies of ***Elder Tales.***

Please add $2.00 per book for postage and handling. Idaho residents include 5% state sales tax in the amount of $.65 per book. Send check payable to:

Historic Idaho, Inc.
P.O. Box 4534
Boise, Idaho 83711

Print Name ____

Address ____

City __________________________ State ________ Zip ___________

Elder Tales $12.95 x ___ # books = ________

Postage and Handling $2.00 x ___ # books = ________

Idaho Tax $0.65 x ___ # books = ________

Enclosed is my check/money order
for the total amount of $ ________

Make checks payable to:

Historic Idaho, Inc.

To order by phone, or for bulk discount prices, please call:
(208) 342-7929
Please photo copy this page if additional forms are needed.